God's Child

Memoirs and Philosophy of Life

Terrence Steven Lake

Author's Tranquility Press

ATLANTA, GEORGIA

Terrence Steven Lake/Author's Tranquility Press
3900 N Commerce Dr. Suite 300 #1255
Atlanta, GA 30331, USA
www.authorstranquilitypress.com

Ordering Information:
Quantity sales. Special discounts are available on quantity purchases by corporations, associations, and others. For details, contact the "Special Sales Department" at the address above.

God's Child: Memoirs and Philosophy of Life/Steven Lake
Hardback: 978-1-964362-76-2
Paperback: 978-1-964362-17-5
eBook: 978-1-964362-74-8

To all of God's children.

Acknowledgement

I would like to give my sincere thanks to my sisters-in-law, Marilyn Lake and Alanna Porter; my sister, Cynthia Scoggins ; and Valerie Wilson, for their long hours of typing and retyping the manuscript into a presentable form for the publisher.

Introduction

I wrote this book because I want the people to see that what happened in my life can happen to almost anyone, no matter who he or she may be. Life was created for a purpose, and that purpose was for each and every person to experience life as an individual. Mankind has never been on the right track because his mind wasn't developed. The majority was always looking up to the sky for the answer, when the answer has always been down here on planet Earth: to be free from all and to prepare for the future.

The purpose of this book is to show the people on planet Earth that there is a reason for all of the different races that were put here. And until that purpose is fulfilled, the people who have not been enlightened to the relationship of the universal humanhood will always be a threat to peace on earth and good will toward people.

We have been working our way toward heaven ever since the first day we were put on Earth, and we will continue to do so until each and every human being is self-sufficient.

God's Child

Chapter 1

I was born on July 18, 1947. My mother's name was Juanita, and my father's name was Willie. I had an older sister named Cynthia, who was born on August 24, 1946. I was born in the house that my parents were living in.

My father was born in the South. He had an eighth-grade education, and he came from an average family. I never knew much about my father's past because we were never close. He left my mother when I was three years old. At the time, my mother had three children. My brother Robert was two years old when Dad left.

Four years later, my father remarried, and then my half-brother Willie James Lake Jr. was born. The following year another half-brother, Jesse James Lake, was born. Five years after that, my father had another child, Beverly, by one of his lady friends.

I remember my mother and how difficult it was for her to raise three kids without a job. My father seldom came around or gave my mother money to feed and clothe us. My mother hosted gambling parties to help pay the rent and put food on the table. Gambling parties were common in those days. Everyone in the neighborhood knew each other, and when the weekend came, parents would get together and decide who would give the party for the coming weekend. The person who gave the party would benefit with a percentage of each gambling pot. When my mother's parties did not work out right, her take amounted to very little, and she would not have enough money to pay the bills. There were days when bread and syrup were all we ate.

When I was five years old, I started kindergarten at Dickinson Elementary School. I enjoyed school because it was different. Two of my best friends were in the same grade as me: Carl Hubbard and my cousin Robert Wilson. After school, we would meet in our neighborhood and play together until it was time to go home and go to bed. We did not worry about going home to eat, because most of the time we did not like what was for dinner.

Even though Mom couldn't always do her best for us in the kitchen, she would always do her utmost to teach us right from wrong. I tried to listen to what she would say, but sometimes my friends influenced me into doing things my mother had told me not to do. My friends and I were a very adventurous group of boys. Mom always wanted me to stay close to home, but on some summer mornings, my friends and I would wake up earlier than usual and take a long walk to the forbidden railroad tracks. Once at a crossing, we would decide which way we would go. We never did anything really wrong or destructive, but sometimes we would get involved in rock-throwing contests. Competition was big with us when we were away from our homes.

During one of our long walks, my friends and I decided to take an unfamiliar route away from the railroad tracks. We walked for two hours and then came upon a swampy pond. The sky was clear, and the sun was directly over our heads. We decided to stay and make a raft. We found what looked like an old door. I suggested that we try floating on it, but it sank. We looked for something else that would float. Carl Hubbard found a big log that was used for support of the railroad tracks. We put it into the water, and it floated. We rode it for a while, until we discovered there were tadpoles in the water. We found some tin cans and filled them with water and tadpoles. After we were tired of playing in the water, we dried off, gathered our treasury of tin cans and tadpoles, and started for home. We walked for an hour and then we came to a cross street. The street looked familiar, and we figured that if we followed it, we would get to our homes.

The day was getting hotter, and we stopped to rest. Carl spotted an apple tree in someone's backyard. We could see the apples from where we were sitting in the alley. (Whenever we traveled on foot, we went through the alleys.) We climbed onto the barn next to the apple tree and picked the apples from there. When we each had about four or five apples, we climbed down and continued our journey home.

When we spotted the Chrysler Plant Dodge Main, we knew we were near home. Carl and Robert had already eaten all their apples Mickey had two left, and I had one. Before we split to go home, we made plans to return to that creek again.

That was one of those days I will never forget. We woke early in the morning to make that trip. It was a feeling of freedom, of having not care in the world.

I was seven years old when my mother met Sherman Holmes Jr. We called him Bill. A year or so after Mom and Bill met, my brother Sherman Michael Holmes was born. Bill was living with us then. He had come from Mississippi to Detroit to get a job. He was from a large family with three boys and five girls. You couldn't have met a better person. Everybody loved him.

On July 12, 1957, my sister Leslie Holmes was born.

I was a youngster myself when Mother felt that I should accept some of the responsibilities for my brothers and sisters. By the time I was eleven, I could do anything around the house that a fifteen-year-old boy could.

On May 9, 1959, my sister Desiree Kimberly Holmes was born. Things were getting tougher at home. Life was hard for everyone in those days. There were a few families in the neighborhood that didn't send their kids to school for the first few weeks because the kids didn't have anything decent to wear. A child would get embarrassed if he or she couldn't start school with new clothes. After the beginning weeks, it would not make any difference, and the child would go to school.

Chapter 2

During some of the clear summer nights of my youth, I slept on the front porch on the second floor of our home. Some nights I wouldn't go to sleep because I would be looking for the falling stars that I had heard of. One night I saw one, but it fell only so far and then disappeared. That really puzzled me. I've been looking for another one ever since.

A few nights after I saw that so-called falling star, I went to bed around 2:00 a.m. While I was asleep, I had a dream that I had gotten out of bed and gone to the back porch. When I looked out the window, I saw four or five moons outside. It seemed so real that I didn't tell any of my friends; they would have made fun of me, and I probably would have been embarrassed.

In my later years, around the end of 1973, I read a couple of books on astronomy. In both, I found out that the planet Saturn has nine moons revolving around it and three huge rings encircling it. The planet Mars has two moons. The planet Jupiter has twelve moons, and the planet itself is over 1,300 times the size of planet Earth. There are five other planets in our solar system, as most of you know, but for those who don't know and want to study up on them, I'll let you have the pleasure in seeking the information.

During those summer years from the ages of nine to thirteen, I would get up in the morning and rush straight over to the next block to meet my friends at an old abandoned house, so we could decide which sport we would play or what we would do for that day. Most of the time we would end up playing strike-out, a baseball game that only required four guys to play, with two on each team. One man would pitch the ball, and the other would catch the ball and call the strikes or balls according to his own judgment. There wasn't a ballpark in our neighborhood, so we played in the alley or in a vacant lot.

There were three particular weeks in the summer when we had a chance to get most of the guys in the neighborhood to participate in the original game of baseball. On my street was a gravel parking lot that belonged to the plant where I was employed. Three weeks in the summer, the plant would close up shop and send almost all of its employees on vacation. We kids really took advantage of it. There were probably only three or four days out of the three weeks that we didn't have one or more baseball games there, with the full nine players on both teams and several other guys on the sidelines wanting to play. Sometimes we had so much fun playing that the games would last until it became so dark that we could hardly see the ball. When the three weeks were up, the only times we had a chance to have the full-scale games were on Saturdays and Sundays.

During those weekdays when we didn't play baseball, there were other sports that occupied our time––basketball or "alley ball," for instance. We couldn't afford an official basketball rim, so we would save all of the wooden bushel baskets we could find and nail them one at a time on the side of a barn; we cut the bottoms out of the baskets to make them into rims. The reason I say one at a time is because each one would last only one or two days. Nailing the baskets on the barns went on for a couple of years until one of us discovered that if we nailed the basket on one of the poles in the alley that had a light connected to it, it would give us a chance to play basketball half the night.

During my junior high and high school years, I won three basketball trophies playing in a recreation league at school. In junior high I played football in the eighth grade. I also ran cross country in ninth grade and played baseball in the tenth grade.

I was educated on religion in a Presbyterian church. From when I was eight until I was twelve, there were a group of mostly white students from a local college that worked with our church during the summer. They would come into our neighborhood and teach the children crafts, take us on trips, and even buy paint and repair some of the houses that needed it. They brought a lot of harmony to our neighborhood. The people were happy and close to one another. I don't know what happened to those people. Their spirit is desperately needed today.

We had a white pastor who had a beautiful mind. I always respected him. During our Sunday services, he would teach us different parts of the Bible. There were some things the church taught that I didn't understand. However, what he taught, I believed was righteous.

I would sit in the front of the church most of the time because I wanted to hear what our pastor was talking about. When he spoke of God, I used to visualize God as a man, a person that was so huge that he could see the whole world and everybody in it at the same time. Sometimes it would frighten me, because whenever I made a mistake or did something wrong, I felt that God was watching me. There were sometimes when I knew I was going to do something wrong, but my mind was so set, so involved, that I didn't even think of God.

If I did something wrong and my mother heard that I was involved, she would look me right in the eyes and ask me what happened. She knew it if I lied, and she punished me for it. If I told the truth, she knew it, and if she thought I deserved to be punished, she would punish me. Now that I have children of my own, I understand why she did the things she did. Knowing what happened then, I can try to prevent my children from making the same mistakes. I know all they want is love and care.

I liked hanging around the older boys in the neighborhood. They liked me being around them, which was good and bad. I acquired a lot of knowledge from them. They took me places I had never been, and they gave me nickels and dimes when I asked for them. They even taught me how to fight to protect myself. I was also exposed to the bad language that they would use sometimes. I wasn't aware of the meaning of some of the words; I had never heard them at home, and my young friends never spoke them. But these words! When you heard them, you couldn't forget them.

The older I got, the more I heard those words. I began to think they were a part of our language, until I got mad at my brother Robert one day and said, "Goddamnit, I'm gonna beat your ass." He told my mother. She came into the bedroom and asked me what I said, and I knew by the way she looked at me and the tone of her voice that I had said something wrong. I hesitated to give an answer, but she demanded I tell her, and I did. She scolded me and told me never to use those words again, and then she whipped me. I thought afterward about what I had said, and I wondered who made those words. But that wasn't the last time I would say those words. Those words and many more became common language in the world of my friends, but I never again spoke to them in my mother's house.

When I was eleven years old, the father and an uncle of a white friend of mine who lived in the neighborhood (which was one of the few white families) organized a Boy Scout group. I had heard many things about the Boy Scouts: they took trips, went camping in the woods, and took long hikes. I knew I would enjoy being one because I was a very adventurous boy. When I found out the day that the first Scout meeting was going to be held, I went and told all my black friends in the neighborhood.

On the day of the first meeting, there were about eight black boys and four white ones sitting in a large room, waiting impatiently to see what the Boy Scouts were all about. The meeting wasn't long. The Scoutmasters just wanted to see if they could get enough boys from our neighborhood. Everyone who was there signed a list stating that they would become an active member.

After the meeting was over, we went out into the hall, where a Coke machine was located, and everyone bought a Coke. Everyone had money that night, because to us that was a very special affair. Even if we didn't have a chance to spend it, it was a great feeling being around your friends with change in your pockets.

We started meeting once a week on Thursdays. At each meeting we heard lectures on the duties of a Boy Scout, memorized the slogans, and got acquainted with all the different material we would need. There was the uniform with accessories we were required to have, which soon posed a problem for some of the members. Six members dropped out because of the lack of money in the household. I was fortunate; my mother gave me my uniform as a Christmas gift. She knew how much I enjoyed belonging to the Scouts, and she even managed to buy the books that were required. Yes, my mother always tried to give us what she felt we really would benefit from in the present and future.

Winter weather was taking its time breaking into spring. This was when our troop raised money by selling fresh doughnuts door to door early in the morning. These Saturday mornings were very mild and refreshing ones. You could still see the dew coating all Mother Nature's plant life. You couldn't help but notice the beautiful shades of blue in this vast ocean of sky, with an occasional fluffy cotton-soft cloud drifting across it.

By selling doughnuts, plus conducting a few other fundraising drives, we accumulated enough money in our treasury to help us take outings during the coming summer. It seemed as though summer would never arrive. When it did, we had prepared ourselves for a three-day weekend camping trip up north. We were to join several other Scout troops for the annual camping event.

I remember now the night before the trip I couldn't sleep at all. I tossed and turned all night, trying to imagine the outing. When the sun rose in the morning, I got up before the clock sounded its alarm, and I went into the dining room to double-check my equipment and make sure nothing had been left out. I noticed my brother had gotten up and was coming toward the dining room to see me off. He was still half- asleep, so he plopped down in one of the dining room chairs, watching me through eyes that were set half-mast and yet eyes of anticipation of being able to take this same trip one day. My mother had prepared lunch for me, but I was sure I would be too excited to eat it.

Before going to the Scoutmaster's home, where everyone was to meet, I had to pick up my black friend, who by now was waiting patiently. At last, I couldn't believe we had finally started on our three- hour journey to the campgrounds. To me, that was a very long time to imagine what our destiny had in store for us.

When we arrived, all the other Boy Scouts had their uniforms on. I was looking forward to getting out of the car to show off my uniform. We saw a pond where a group of Scouts were fishing. About one hundred yards from the pond were the cabins, where our nights were to be spent. When I got out of the car and stretched my arms out, I took a deep breath of fresh, clean air— and I mean fresh air. After we had taken everything out of the station wagon and straightened up the cabin, it was time to eat lunch. When we finished eating lunch, everyone was exhausted.

We rested for a while, and then the Scoutmasters told us a list of things we would be doing. We had a ball the whole time we were there. I can remember looking up into the sky and night and seeing an unimaginable amount of stars in the sky.

After our weekend camping trip, it wasn't very long before the whole troop broke up, for what reason I really don't know. However, I will never forget the one slogan: "On my honor, I will do my best, to do my duty to God and my country, and to obey the Scout law, to help other people at all times, to keep myself physically strong, mentally awake, and morally straight."

I really enjoyed being a Boy Scout. It taught me many things that I probably would have never learned in everyday city life. We learned how to read a compass, how to tie different kinds of knots with a rope, how to conduct ourselves as young men instead of boys, how to apply first aid to an injured person, and how to respect and help our fellow men. I would recommend that every young man or boy join a boys' club or Scout troop to get a more constructive relationship with his fellow brothers and become more aware of the country life.

School was beautiful. I went to an integrated school, and I felt that it was very beneficial for my understanding of the world today. When I was in the fourth grade, I began to understand some of the different personalities I encountered in my classes. I got a chance to play with kids from a different environment.

When I went into a class for the first time, I would sit there and not say a word. I would pick a kid out that I thought had the same type of personality as mine. I would start a conversation by asking him his name, and then I would start talking about sports. After that we would become good classroom friends. I didn't have any of my own neighborhood friends in my classes from the fourth through the sixth grade. I would see my neighborhood friends only at lunchtime or while passing through the halls during change of classes. I met white Robert Kinsmen while we were both in the fourth grade. He was very quiet and hardly talked to anyone in school. He was a very nice student in class and got very good grades. I believe I was probably one of the few guys he would talk to.

In the fourth grade I became aware of my mathematical ability. I really enjoyed math. It was my best subject all the way through school. Sometimes I wondered if I was gifted in math or if I excelled in it because of my fourth-grade math teacher. She was an elderly white woman with a very warm heart. Every time I walked into her class or saw her, I felt the warm vibrations. She loved math and taught it with enthusiasm.

The summer after fourth grade, I began to notice that some of the people who were in my classes would hang around some of the parks in the city and were passing through my neck of the woods. It was nice knowing people other than those you grew up with. I knew how to go places other than in my neighborhood to have a good time. And I knew that when I went to junior high school, I would know how to get there without anyone's guidance.

In junior high school I met more people; I relished knowing the school athletes, who my sister told me about. I felt I was growing up. I was delighted, going more places than I had ever dreamed of. In school I was having a hard time in my English class. My math and other classes were okay. I believe English was a rough subject for me because I was used to communicating in my own neighborhood language, which was not proper English.

Junior high school only had two grades: seventh and eighth. Those two years went by so fast that I can hardly remember what was going on during that time. Graduation time was coming up before I could even think of it. It was beautiful. I had the feeling of going to a bigger school. In the summer of 1961, my mother made arrangements for my brother Robert and I to spend a thirty-day vacation at a summer camp called the Christmas Seal Camp. The first day of camp started at the end of June. I had been to camp before for two weeks, when I was much younger, and it was a thrill of a lifetime to go away for a couple of weeks and live a life where there was something to do almost every minute of the day—and I got to eat three full meals every day. This particular camp accommodated the boys and girls at the same time. Naturally, the girls had their own cabins and the boys had theirs, and the supervision was fantastic. The whole lot of us was just like one big family, with approximately fifty kids.

Both camps were integrated. The only problems that the counselors had were child's play. The camps were similar in that in both of them everything was preplanned.

We went swimming every day, or you might say some of us went swimming and some of us played in the water. They did teach most of us how to swim before our thirty days were over. I tried so hard to swim, but I could only travel about ten feet. I was one of the oldest boys there, and I felt very embarrassed when watching some of the little seven-year-old boys stroking through the water like fish. There were markers in the water that divided the non-swimmers from the swimmers. During certain times of the day, there were counselors at the lake who arranged the swimmers in groups. You were either a fish, which meant you were a very good swimmer; a minnow, which meant that you could swim well enough to save your life; or a rock, which meant you couldn't swim at all.

I was a rock, but it didn't last long. After a week I became a minnow. The test that we had to take to become a minnow was swimming about twenty yards. You had to swim across the width of the lake if you wanted to become a fish, and the lake was only a fourth of a mile wide. Swimming across the lake was a real challenge for me. Day after day I stroked desperately, trying to build up my confidence so that I would accept the challenge. Two weeks after becoming a minnow, I accepted the challenge. The day I started my voyage across the lake, I didn't try to see if my brother or any other friends were watching. I had only one thing on my mind—and that was to swim across the lake.

When a person wanted to swim across the lake, the counselors got a ten-foot pole and a rowboat. They rowed about fifteen feet in front of the swimmer the whole time, unless he or she needed help.

When I started out, I tried freestyle swimming for about a fourth of the way. I then turned over on my back and tried the back stroke. When I became tired, I turned over onto my side and started the side stroke. This was a relaxed position for me. I continued in that position until I thought I had enough strength to swim freestyle again.

When I started freestyle, I could tell that I had swum across over three-fourths of the lake. I began swimming faster, thinking that I would get to the shore sooner, but it didn't turn out that way. I became so tired that I had to stop swimming and tread water to catch my breath. I could see that I had only about twenty-five yards to go. I started thinking about what would happen if I couldn't make it the rest of the way across or get to the boat. Before I knew it, the boat had gotten more than the twenty-foot limit away, and I panicked. The counselors noticed my strange actions. They stuck the pole out toward me and came close so that I could grab the pole.

When I climbed into the boat, I thought I had just gotten saved from drowning, but it really wasn't that bad. If I had just kept on swimming, I would have made it to the shore without thinking about it.

On the way back to the other side of the lake, where I had started, the counselors gave me some words of encouragement. They told me that I could always try again. I was so disappointed, but I knew I had accomplished something. Swimming over three-fourths of the way was really a success to me, considering that I had started as a rock.

I had so much fun while I was at camp that it became fun going to bed at night, knowing that I had another exciting day ahead of me. One day we went on a ten-mile hike, and when we reached our destination, we camped overnight in tents. In the morning when we woke up, we had to use well water to wash up.

For breakfast we cooked the food over a pile of burning wood, tree limbs, paper, and anything else that would burn. It seemed as though the breakfast that we helped prepare tasted better than some of the breakfasts we had back at the cabin.

Everything went perfectly while I was at camp, except for one particular evening after supper. The cabin that I slept in was one of the homes for the older boys at the camp, and the cabin that my brother Robert slept in was for the next oldest group. There were about eight cabins that were occupied with boys. I had two very close friends that I spent most of my time with. I can't remember their names, but one was black and the other was white; I'll call them Black and White.

After supper that particular day, Black, White, and I were lying around, thinking of something to do while our counselors were at a special meeting. As we were deciding what to do, we were looking through our cabin window and directly into my brother's cabin. It looked like they were having fun. I thought it would be fun for us to go over there and scare them.

Black, White, and I slipped out of our cabin and approached my brother's cabin. A few other guys from our cabin followed us over there, and before I knew it, the scare we had planned turned out to be a wrestling match. We were in my brother's cabin, throwing the older boys all over the place. I just happened to look out of the window, and I saw my counselor standing outside, watching everything that was going on. When I stopped, everyone else stopped and began running out the door. I ran as well.

About fifteen minutes later, my counselor called me into his office. He asked me what happened, and I didn't say anything. He asked me again, and I said something smart. Before I knew what was going on, he had snatched me off my feet and held me in the air upside down, beating the hell out of me. I cried and cried. I cried because of the pain and from embarrassment. But it did teach me a lesson, and I didn't get any other wild ideas.

When our thirty days were over and it was time to go home, the strangest feeling in my life ran through my body. I knew what it was, but I didn't want to let it come out. I knew that I probably would never see Black and White, my counselor, and the rest of the boys again, and that made me sad. It was time to go home, so I took one long last look at the place as the bus drove away.

Black was on the bus with my brother and me, but White's parents came to take him home. That camp adventure was one that I will never forget.

Chapter 3

When I started going to high school, I began to realize how I had neglected my English homework. When I got to the eleventh grade, it was almost too late, but I managed to get by.

In August 1964, my cousin and I rode the bus to the Michigan State Fair. It was a very warm day, and the fairgrounds were packed with people. My cousin and I were at the teenage fair inside a large fenced-in area, where you had to pay extra to get in. We had just watched Martha and the Vandellas perform, and we were walking around. We stopped when we saw two white girls looking into a mirror. My cousin said, "You're looking good." They smiled, and one of them answered, "Thank you." We stood there for a few minutes and then started walking again. All of a sudden, a man with his arm in a cast came up to us and asked if I wanted to be an Indian. I told him to get out of my way; he pointed a green stick with paint on it, at me and again asked, "Do you want to be an Indian?" I noticed that about fifteen other guys, all white except for one Mexican, had surrounded us. The Mexican pulled a knife. Out of instinct, I ran in the opposite way of the knife––I was running for my life. I saw a group of black brothers, and I ran their way. They saw what was happening and came to my rescue. Someone from the white group threw a bottle into our crowd, and glass broke. Before I knew it, there were policemen on horseback riding through the crowd, trying to break up the fight.

Everyone began to run, trying to get out of the way of the horses. As I was running toward the gate, one of the policemen hit the top of my head so hard that it broke his club. I immediately fell and hit the ground. The policeman got off his horse and grabbed me as I was getting up.

He took out his handcuffs and put them on my wrists. He squeezed so hard that the mark was on my wrists for a week. He knocked a hole in my head the size of a nickel, and there was so much blood on my face that I could hardly see. The police walked me through the crowd to the back of the fairgrounds. I thought I was going to bleed to death before I reached where we were going.

We reached a building under the grandstands behind the racetrack, where there were more police standing around. The policeman took me inside and told me to sit down. I was so mad that I just stood there crying, staring at him. He got mad and pushed me over the chair. When I fell on the floor, he picked me up and pushed me into the wall and put his knee in my back. There were other policemen standing around, including a black one. No one would help me. Finally, they brought a police wagon to take me to the first-aid building, where they patched my head.

The police then took me to the Receiving Hospital and chained me to a bed. I waited seven hours before I was taken to surgery for stitching. Later, I was then taken back to the station near the fairgrounds and locked up until my mother got me out the next day.

When they let me out of jail the next day, I didn't want to go back to my neighborhood, knowing I would feel embarrassed in front of the neighbors. I felt as though I was a criminal after being locked up in jail. I had a lot of hate in me. I wanted to get even with that policeman, but I knew I would never get even because he was on the side of the law; I would just get into deeper trouble if I tried anything foolish. That ended up being one of the key lessons I learned in my life.

I thought my world was coming to an end. Everyone in my neighborhood had heard what had happened before it was put into the papers. On the way home from jail, my mother told me not to worry about anything. She said that everything would be all right. I was still a little frightened, because I had heard how the police could put people in jail for crimes they didn't commit. Just the thought of going back to jail scared the hell out of me.

When we reached home, there were friends waiting for me at my house. My cousin told them what had happened, and a lot of my friends decided to go to the fair that day to see if anything else was going to break out. All the older people in the neighborhood were very upset over what had happened, and some of them called me over to their porch to show me their concern. This made me feel better, knowing that they were in my corner and not thinking that I was just a troublemaker.

The next day my name was in the paper. A whole column in the paper reported that I had incited a riot. I wanted to cry. I knew people would read it and think that the paper was telling the truth. Fortunately, the charges were dropped, and I didn't have to go to court. For a long time people questioned me about what had happened, and I had to explain it over and over again. I felt like I would hate white people for the rest of my life.

In September when school started, I was embarrassed for the first couple of weeks because I had a bald spot on the top of my head. I tried to cover the spot with my hair, but my hair wasn't long enough. A few people made fun of it, but eventually they forgot about it.

This was my last year in school, and I was able to have all the fun I could imagine, while keeping my grades above average. Instead of hating the white people, some of them became some of my best friends. I started going to parties with a group of them and riding up and down the main street in Hamtramck with them. We became very close. Whenever there was some kind of sports affair that took place out of town, I always had one or more ways of getting there. There were only a few black guys who had a car of their own, and if you wanted to ride with them, you had to put on a skirt, makeup, and a wig. Most of the black and white students in school got along very well, but outside of school, everyone went his or her own way. When I started hanging around the white guys, I lost all but a few close friends.

During that last year in high school, I hung around the poolroom half a block from school. This was the spot where most of my friends met during lunch hour or after school. That's where I would win my lunch money.

One day after school I was standing outside the poolroom, trying to decide if I should go home and get money or wait for a friend of mine who owed me three dollars from a previous game. As I waited, Tom, a white classmate, walked up and asked me if I wanted to shoot a game. I said, "I don't have any money, but if you'll be here when I get back, I'll shoot some games with you."

"If you're going to come right back, can I go with you?" he asked.

I hesitated, thinking, *Why does he want to come over my house?* But then I said, "Well, if you want to."

He said, "Yeah."

When we reached my house, I thought about what my mother might think, knowing what had happened that summer at the fair. She was cooking dinner when she saw us come in the back door. She stopped, and I introduced her to Tom.

"Would you like to have dinner with us?" she asked.

"Yes, thank you," Tom said.

I said, "Well, you can come into the front room with me and watch television until supper is ready."

After we ate, we went back to the poolroom. There were two tables vacant, and we got one. I only had a dollar, and I lost it. I was hoping that my friend who owed me the money would show up, but he didn't. Tom said he'd pay for a couple of games, and we shot for another hour, until Tom was broke.

"Well, I guess I'll see you tomorrow," Tom said.

"Okay, man, later."

That was when I started hanging out with my white friends.

That next day in school, I saw Tom between classes. He came over to me and started rapping about going to the poolroom again. As the bell rang, I said I'd see him after school. "Where you going?" he asked.

I said, "I have to go to chorus." He caught up to me and walked me to my class, rapping all the way. In class I wondered why he was so nice to me.

As the weeks went by, Tom and I became closer and closer. One Friday night, Tom came into the poolroom and asked me if I wanted to go to a party with him. Without thinking I said, "Yeah." We had to walk, and when we got a few houses from the party, I thought, *what in the hell am I doing? There probably won't be any blacks there. Well, it will be in Hamtramck; if anything happens, I know where to go and who to get.*

When we went into the house, no one said anything good or bad, but a few guys looked at me in a strange way. During the party, a couple of guys who I knew came in, and when they saw me, they came over to me with big smiles on their faces and started rapping. I had a good time at that party. It was a new experience for me. A few weeks went by, and I got to know more guys by going to more parties. I didn't worry about anything because those friends of mine knew me and I knew them.

There was a party coming up at a hall in Hamtramck that most of the white guys talked about for weeks. I didn't rap about it because I wasn't hip to what was going on. A week before the party started, I was invited to go. It was at the PNA hall, the Polish National Alliance Hall. The night of the party I got dressed sharp and waited at my house for some of the guys to pick me up. Since there was about an hour before the party started, we rode to a store, and everyone chipped in to get some wine and beer. There were five of us in the car, and we bought four bottles of wine and a case of beer. We didn't drink it all, but we did drink most of it before we went into the dance. We had to pay to get into the dance. I noticed as we entered that there were quite a few people. I looked around to see if I knew anyone there, and I did see a number of people I knew from school. I even saw a couple of black girls there.

They wouldn't dance with me, but you know how that is.

During the course of the night, as I was standing in a large room where they served refreshments, a fight broke out between a friend of mine and another guy. While they were exchanging blows, I saw a huge Mexican friend of mine named Billy come running through the crowd, jump on a table, and hit the fellow who was fighting my other friend. The punch was square in the nose. Blood shot everywhere, and the stranger fell to the floor. Another friend of mine grabbed me by the arm and said to get out of there because of the police.

I followed him to the car, and Billy was already sitting in the car with the other three friends I came with. By the time we got to the car, there were already a couple of police cars looking around. One of the police cars came toward us. When the policeman started to talk to the driver of our car, it seemed to me as though they knew each other. One of my friends sitting in the back with me said, "Wow, that's his brother." Billy was in the Naval Reserves, and all that week he was on active duty. He was supposed to have had a four-hour pass, and I think he only had half an hour to get back to Belle Isle to his submarine. We got him there on time. I never heard the results of that incident, but I know Billy didn't go to jail.

About two weeks after that, I was riding around Hamtramck with my white friends again. A friend of ours named Frank pulled up alongside us and started yelling that a car full of white guys, friends of the stranger Billy had knocked out, were chasing Frank through Hamtramck. We pulled over to the side of the road, and Frank got into our car in order to ride around and find those strangers. We spotted them and chased them through Hamtramck into Detroit, driving down the main street. It was a real chase. They made a quick turn down a side street, and as we followed, turning the corner on two wheels, we ran into a street sign. As we were trying to get out of the car, I noticed that Billy had pulled the steering wheel right out of the socket. We managed to get the steering wheel back into place, but the front bumper had a large dent in it.

We drove over to Billy's house and parked in the alley. We stayed there all night, trying to fix the bumper. Billy's father was in the hospital, so we all called our parents and got permission to spend the night at his house. Naturally we didn't tell our parents what had happened.

It was a month before graduation, and the weather was beautiful. My sister bought me a 1953 Oldsmobile as a graduation present. I picked up one of my white friends and then we drove up and down the main street in Hamtramck. As we rode, I saw four black guys I knew from school getting ready to beat up two white guys, who I also knew. I realized that once those four black guys started fighting those two white guys, it would be a massacre. I thought about what had happened at the State Fair, and I never wanted to see anything like that happen again, to me or anyone else. I yelled out of the car window and told the black guys to give the white ones a break. The black guys were one or two years younger than me, and they knew me. They heard what I said, and they halted their attempted attack on the white guys. The next day in school, there were a few black guys going around threatening to jump on some of the white guys. A couple of my white friends told me that they were threatened and that the black guys who threatened them said they were going to get me too. During school hours, I saw two of the black guys I had stopped from fighting, and they told me that they were going to get me after school. My response was, "Hey, man! Wait a minute. You know you guys would have beat the hell out of those two white boys. You saw how scared they were."

"What the hell you doing trying to tell us what to do?" they said.

"I know what you were going through. I went through the same thing. All you would have done was get yourself in trouble. I wanted to stop you and tell you that wasn't the way," I said.

The heavy guy in the group responded flatly, "Fuck you! We'll see you after school." They left.

I knew that if I didn't wait after school, they would probably get together with a lot more guys, and then things would really get out of hand. I waited in my car for them. Robert Kinsman was in the car with me. I tried to get some of my close black friends to make sure it would be a fair fight, but they said no. Robert and I waited ten minutes after the school bell rang, but no one else showed up. Robert became impatient and said, "Come on; let's get out of here." I knew he wasn't going to fight, but I had him there to drive my car away so they wouldn't tear it up.

At last I saw them, all of them. There were at least fifteen. Robert shouted, "Let's go; here they come."

I said, "We got to get it over with now." As they approached the car, I tried to get out, but one of them held the door closed, and then another tore the antenna off my car. I saw one of them come toward the car from the back with a long stick. I tried to roll up the window, but it was too late. He punched me in the head with a stick before I could get it up. I pushed the stick out of the car, and another guy kicked my side window out. I had had enough then. My car was already running, so I just put it in drive and drove away.

When I took Robert Kinsman home, I felt like a fool to have sat in the car, letting black guys jump on me because I had protected white guys. Deep down inside, however, I knew I was right. I didn't want to go home. I just wanted to drive as far as I could to get away from it all, but I didn't know where to go. As I got near home, I decided that I would tell my mother that I had a fight, but I wouldn't tell her I was protecting some white guys.

When I told her, she said, "When are you going to learn that fighting doesn't accomplish anything?" I looked at her like the fool I was and didn't say anything. She shook her head and walked away.

That next day in school, I saw the black guys who I had had the fight with. They didn't say anything to me, and I didn't say anything to them. As far as I was concerned, it was over.

I didn't go to my last class that day. Robert and I decided to go for a ride. We got into my car and split away from school. While we were driving, I spotted a car full of black guys going toward our school. When they spotted us, they changed direction and started coming toward us. When they reached my car, they tried to run me off the road. Well, I made sure they wouldn't have a second chance. I drove to the other side of town.

I tried to get back to school before the students got out for the day, but I was too late. When we arrived at school, most of the students had gone home. There were two police cars in front of the school, and some students were standing around. We found out later that the black guys who had run me off the road were from Detroit, and they were looking for some of the black guys that I had the misunderstanding with. The guys from Detroit didn't catch the guys they were looking for, so they caught another black guy and almost cut his ear off. I knew the guy who was cut, and he wasn't what you call a troublemaker. I just couldn't understand them. Why would someone do something like that? I never found out what happened to those guys from Detroit. That was another one of my life experiences

Chapter 4

Time passed. Graduation came and was gone. It left me out in the big world alone. I didn't want to work that summer. All I wanted to do was travel and take it easy, and then I would find a job and start my lifetime career. Unfortunately, I didn't have the money to travel, and sitting around doing nothing without money was miserable. I woke up from that dream and decided to seek employment two weeks after school was out.

The first place that I went for a job was the downtown Michigan Consolidated Gas Company. I took tests and passed them, and they offered me a job driving a mail truck from Detroit to Battle Creek, Michigan, twice a day. However, when I had my interview, they told me I was too young for the job, so they offered me a mail clerk job. I was turned down again because I didn't have enough experience. They said if anything came up, they would call me, but I never heard from them again. I was very disappointed. I didn't get that job on account of my lack of experience, but how could you have experience when you've only been out of school for a couple of weeks?

I went to a couple of other places, but they weren't hiring. I didn't want to go to the factory because of the rumors I had heard and because of the state of mind that some of my friends were in who were working at the factory. I decided to wait for a couple of days and go looking again. The next week, I was getting ready to leave the house, and a young white man came to my door. He asked me if my brother Robert was home. I told him he wasn't. He then asked if I was interested in a job. I knew that the factory employers didn't come to your house to look for you, so I felt safe. I told him I was. He gave me a brochure with information about the job and where it was located. It sounded interesting. It was a government project under the direction of the Mayor's Youth Employment Project (MYEP). The purpose was to recruit eighty guys, who were dropouts from high school and recent graduates from high school. For the first couple of weeks we were supposed to be separated into groups and have a daily schedule of playing sports, listening to lectures, and getting to know each other. After that we were supposed to go up north and pick pickles for eight weeks.

When the man left, I called Carl and a couple of other friends and told them about it. The following week, we joined the project. It was exciting meeting new friends, playing sports, and having rap sessions. The money we received wasn't much, but it was a very enjoyable summer.

Four weeks passed, and we were still doing what we had been doing the first couple of weeks. Around the fifth week, the leaders separated us up into different groups. The high school graduates were placed into one group together, ten of us. The rest of the guys were divided up into different groups, where they were to learn how to fill out applications for future employment; brush up on their math; and be told how to conduct classes in auto repair, reading, etc.

An instructor from Washington, DC, spoke to our group and taught us how to improve our memory and pass apprenticeship tests. It was challenging. It reminded me of the tests we had taken in school. I was the number-one student in the apprenticeship tests and near the top in everything else.

After a couple of months in the MYEP, the leaders decided to take us up north to see where we would pick the pickles. We rode up there on a rented Detroit Streets & Rails bus. It was a long ride, and we had a ball on the way up. We reached our destination, which looked like a slave plantation. There were two abandoned army barracks and acres of green-looking plants that might have been pickle plants. Inside the barracks, it looked like a disaster area. We walked around, and judging by the conversation, most of the guys were not going to return to pick the pickles. We had a hot dog roast and refreshments, and then we *ran* to the bus.

A couple of weeks passed. Some of the guys were placed on jobs outside the program and some had dropped out. Our classes were over, and one of the counselors set us up with appointments for apprenticeship tests at factories. I didn't like the idea of going to the factory, but knowing that it was a skilled trade, I went. A group of us went to Cadillac and Ford to take the tests. I passed all of them, but I didn't get a job and was placed on a waiting list.

I continued to go to the MYEP and collect the checks, until I became bored with it. There weren't that many guys left, and the program didn't accept anyone after the first three weeks. While I was there, I would rap with the counselors about their occupations and a number of other things. They were dedicated men because they caught hell from the guys who were involved in the program, who were almost all hard-core blacks. I found out from one of the counselors that two of them were studying medicine. I had a strange feeling that they were studying us because we never did go and pick pickles, and they kept a close eye on us, recording what we did.

I got tired of going to the MYEP and sitting around doing nothing, so I decided to get a better job. The first job was a factory job. They worked me twelve hours the first day. When I got home, I lay down across my bed and fell asleep. Before I knew it, my mother was waking me up and telling me that it was time to get ready for work again. That lasted for three days, and then I quit. I couldn't see myself working six days a week, twelve hours a day, and sleeping the rest of the time.

A month later I was at another factory, but this time I worked only eight hours, with an hour for lunch and two breaks.

Everything was going beautifully—until I started hanging around some of my old school friends.

Chapter 5

Around the first of November in 1965, I picked up one friend Michael and then drove to another friend's house named Marty, to take them to a party. I'll call the second friend Marty. When we arrived at Marty's house, he wanted us to wait while he drove to the cleaners to pick up something. He left us at his house with his brother, Morice was about two years younger than Marty.

Earlier that day, my sister had rolled my hair in rollers, and before I left the house, I put a hat on that covered all the rollers. While Michael and I were waiting for MARTY Morice saw the funny shape of my head. He walked over and tried to snatch my hat off. I grabbed my hat and held it onto my head. He said, "Let me see your head."

I said, "I've got it in rollers, and I ain't going to take it off."

"You'd better let me see or I'll take it off," he said.

"Hey, man, why don't you be cool? I'm not playing around," I said. I thought he understood, but as soon as I took my eyes off him, he tried to snatch my hat, missing and instead scratching my face. I got mad. I jumped up and grabbed him and wrestled him to the floor. I didn't want to hurt him, so I just held him there. Before I knew it, Marty came into the house and saw me holding his brother on the floor. He didn't hesitate. He jumped on my back and tried to hold me so his brother could get me. While Marty and I were tussling, his brother went in his father's room and came out with a gun. When Michael saw Marty's brother with the gun, he took it from him. By that time, I had control of Marty, and when I saw Michael take the gun, I ran outside. Marty followed, and I thought we were going to have a fair fight, but his brother had gotten another gun and came outside pointing it at me. I ran again, and when I stopped, I saw Marty's little brother had jumped up on the front of my car. He tried to kick my window out. When he didn't succeed, he kicked out one of my side windows.

I really got mad then. I ran toward him, and he came at me, along with Marty. I managed to get into my car and pull out a baseball bat. When they got closer, I ran over to their father's car and knocked the whole back window out. They were still coming, and Marty's brother still had the gun. Michael was standing outside, watching all of this. He couldn't get involved because we were all his friends. I threw Michael the keys to my car and told him to meet me at my house. As I ran down the street, Marty followed me, but I didn't see his brother. I stopped, and as Marty got closer, I went at him and hit him with the bat. His brother appeared, and I disappeared.

When I got home, Michael was there with my car. We went into my house and sat down. While we were sitting, we heard a horn blow. It was Marty and a carload of guys. When some of the guys saw me, I heard one of them say, "That's Lake!" The car pulled off. I took Michael home, and I went back home.

About a week later, I went to a basketball game at school with Michael. After the game, we went over to another friend's house for a party. I had a girlfriend with me, and Michael had one with him. When we arrived at the party, another friend of mine came out on the porch and said, "Marty is in the house." The girl who was with me got frightened and said she didn't want to go in. The friend who lived there said that everything was all right and that there wouldn't be anything happening that night. I assured her that everything would be all right and that Marty wouldn't start anything in someone else's house.

Everyone had a girlfriend at the party except Marty. He sat around talking with different people. We left the party before he did, and I didn't see him until two weeks later.

Three of my friends and I had driven out to River Rouge, Michigan, to see some girls we had met at a Hamtramck football game. We had been out there for three hours and were on our way home when Marty pulled alongside my friend's car. Marty said, "Hey, Lake, I heard you were looking for me."

I said, "Naw, I heard you were looking for me."

He said, "I am. Get out the car." I thought we were going to have a fair fight. I got out of the car. When he came toward me, I saw a gun in one hand and a blackjack in the other. I looked at his eyes, and it appeared to me that he was losing his mind. I didn't know if I should run or what. We both shuffled in a circle, as if we were getting ready to have a fistfight. He hit me with the blackjack, and I reached into my coat pocket and pulled out an empty beer can. I acted as though I was going to throw it, and he ducked. I knew he was going to shoot, so I faked a throw again and threw it. When he ducked, I ran like hell.

I heard shots. I turned around to see if he was coming, and he was right behind me. I couldn't run fast enough. I saw a house that was under construction, and I ran over to it. I picked up a two-by-four laying in the yard and turned around. He was shooting at me and ran out of bullets. When I saw that, I attacked him. Suddenly, I felt that my neck had swollen up. "Lake, you been shot!" shouted Murry I felt my neck but didn't feel or see any blood. I felt it again, and this time I saw blood. I put my whole hand on my jaw and saw more blood. I knew I was shot. Since I couldn't catch Marty, I ran over to his car and started knocking his windows out until he reloaded the gun and came back shooting again. I ran and hid behind a car, and then he ran to his car and pulled away with one of his friends. Murry came over to me and said, "You've been shot. Come on, man; I'm going to take you to the hospital."

When we arrived at the hospital, Michael went up to the desk and said, "My friend has been shot."

I said, "I don't want to die. Somebody do something for me."

The nurse said, "We can take you in, but we can't do anything for you unless you have someone over twenty-one to sign for you."

"You mean to tell me, since I'm not twenty-one, you can't save my life?" I replied. "What the hell is going on? Somebody has got to do something. I don't want to die."

A security guard walked over and said, "I'll sign for him." Looking at me, he said, "You'll be all right, young fellow. Just take it easy."

After that everything went dark. I don't remember anything until I was on an elevator. I remember the small space, the lights, and the door opening. When I regained consciousness, I saw my mother, my father, my sister Cynthia, my cousin Joseph Bevelle, and a girlfriend. I almost forgot what happened, until I felt my neck and jaw. I had stitches in three different places. The holes in my jaw and in the back of my neck were small. A bullet had entered my jaw, and they took it out of the back of my neck, but I couldn't understand why I had such a long scar on the side of my neck. (Later on I was told they thought that the bullet had gone through my gland, so they had to operate and see what damage the bullet had done. They said that if the bullet had been a half-inch closer to my gland, I would have died.) I felt the stitches and thought for a minute, *What will people think when they see me?* Everyone was telling me what they had heard happened and that the police were looking for Marty. I didn't really pay anyone that much attention; I had too many other things on my mind.

When they left, I lay in bed thinking of what I was going to do to Marty. I could hardly sleep. I wanted to get out of bed the first night and go looking for him, but I fell asleep.

The next morning, two detectives came into my room to ask me some questions. They showed me the bullet that came out of my neck. One of the detectives asked if I was going to press charges. I hesitated for a minute, and a thousand thoughts went through my mind. "I don't know. I'll have to think about it more," I said.

After they left, an elderly fellow came over to my bed and said, "Son, you've been saved. You ought to thank God—you've been blessed." I don't remember the other words he said, but I will never forget those few words.

That night, I felt as though I could get out of bed and go looking for X. As the hours passed, I felt that it was either him or me and that I'd better forget what had happened. Still, I knew I could never take my eyes off him again. I knew that it would be worse the next time, and someone might get killed. The next day I was told the police had picked up Marty, but he was out on bail. It really didn't bother me then because I felt the whole situation over.

Later the same day, my family came to see me. When they left, four of my white school friends came in. They told me the different stories each had heard about me. One of them said, "I heard half of your face was blown away." And they told me many more versions of what happened. I got a card from Robert's mother, telling me how she felt and that she wished I would hurry up and get well and come home. Another one of my white friends told me that there were more friends who wanted to come, but they were afraid they might get jumped in that all-black area. After they left, I went into my thoughts again. I thought about all my so-called friends I had grown up with and the phony excuses they would use to explain to me why they couldn't come and see me on my deathbed.

After eight days, I was discharged from the hospital. I had to go to court for the fight. I didn't press charges on Marty. All I wanted him to do was pay for my hospital bill. I didn't want revenge. When Marty's father heard what I said, he wanted to say something to me, but he held it back. I knew that Marty's father was sorrier than his son was, because I had talked with him, and my mother had grown up with him. He was a very respectful person.

On January 7, 1966, I started working at the Ford Motor Company as a millwright apprentice. On January 14, 1966, my brother Shawn Gavin Holmes was born.

When I started at Ford, I was put on the first shift for eight weeks. I didn't get a chance to go to the college for the apprenticeship classes when I first started because it was in the middle of the semester. That was one factory I really enjoyed. Most of the people were friendly, and they went out of their way to help me whenever they could. When the apprentices were on maintenance and had everything running, they could spend their time studying homework or even reading. I don't know if all the Ford plants were like that, but this particular one was.

During those first eight weeks at Ford, I started going to Ecorse on the weekends, to party with some of the guys that I had met in the hospital. That's when I met Jonathan Barnett, better known as J.B.

After eight weeks, I was put on the afternoon shift. Two days out of the week, I attended Henry Ford Community College. After school I went over to J.B.'s house, because he lived only fifteen minutes from Ford and fifteen minutes from the Ford college. J.B. was on the afternoon shift at Ford's too.

J.B. and I had a very exciting time when we were together. We would go to cabarets all over Wayne County. Cabarets were the thing that was happening when I was nineteen years old. If you were under twenty-one, it was the thing to do in order to have a good time. You didn't need any proof to get in. You had to bring your own bottle, and either you bought your tickets in advance and saved fifty cents, or you paid the full price at the door.

One day at work, while I was on the day shift, I was sitting around doing nothing and thought of taking a long trip somewhere. I thought of a lot of places, but I didn't know the way to get to them. I had never left Michigan. The next day I saw my cousin Robert Wilson, and we both talked about going out of town for the weekend. He had been to Chicago a number of times. He knew how to get there without a map. I thought that would be a beautiful place to visit. I had heard a lot of things about Chicago and had seen different pictures of the city. I knew it would be a great experience traveling through the country with a couple of friends. Robert and I agreed that would be the place to go, but we didn't set a date because I wanted to ask J.B. if he would like to go with us. The following day I had to go to school, and when I saw J.B., I asked if he wanted to go to Chicago. He was delighted, so that weekend, J.B., Robert, and I made plans to go to Chicago the following weekend. When Friday came, the day we planned to leave, I felt like an explorer getting ready to go to the moon. J.B. and I didn't go to work that Friday. I got up early and washed my car, and then I got my suitcases and put them into the trunk. I picked up Robert, and then we drove to Ecorse to get to J.B. When he had all his things packed, we were off to Chicago.

We took turns driving, and we stopped only for gas. It took us three and a half hours to get there. When we got there, Robert drove to our aunt's house. She lived in the South Side projects. It was one of the roughest neighborhoods in Chicago. There were a lot of gangs in Chicago. If you were a stranger, you had to be very careful about where you went. If you were white, you definitely didn't belong. If you were black, you had to know someone in the neighborhood. If you didn't know someone and you got caught by the gang, you would get a bad beating.

We stayed at our aunt's house for an hour. When we left the projects, we went to find a place to stay. We drove around in the downtown area of Chicago, with all of the tall buildings, shopping centers, theaters, etc. We went to a big hotel and asked for a room on the top floor. They didn't have one available on the top floor, so they gave us a room about fifteen stories up. There were two beds in the room. We decided to flip to see who would get the single bed, and I won. We showered, changed our clothes, and went to look the town over.

It was dark outside when we left the hotel. The city was lit up beautifully. I saw a subway for the first time. It was just like in the movies. I saw the skyway, which ran over the city. In the ghetto part of the city, under the skyway at nighttime, most people would party on the street. People could walk in that area all night until five o'clock in the morning, and they could find partying crowds everywhere. I don't know how late people stay up now, but that's how it was back then. A lot of the stores were open, and the bars didn't close until five o'clock in the morning. They reopened at 6:00 a.m., an hour later.

We met some girls in the city and made a date to pick them up and take them to the beach. After we picked them up that evening, we stopped at the liquor store and bought three half-pints of whiskey. They didn't bring any food with them, so we also picked up something to eat on the way to the beach. I don't remember if you had to be twenty-one to buy liquor or if you had to be at least eighteen, but we didn't get any static when we bought the alcohol. The girls probably would've brought some food, but by the way they were dressed and what they told us about the conditions in the city, we understood. We had a beautiful time at the beach. It was packed with people. There were some black brothers playing the bongos, and a lot of black brothers and sisters were dancing to the sounds. It didn't occur to me until we were ready to leave that the water was Lake Michigan.

On the way home, we saw a gang of black guys standing on the corner where we were going to let the girls off. I didn't think anything of it, but one of the girls in the backseat said, "That's my boyfriend and his gang." My natural instinct told me to keep on going. When we drove past them, I heard someone holler, "There they go."

I guess I panicked because I drove so fast and so far, that we ended up behind some big plant almost on the outskirts of Chicago. We were lost. No one knew where we were (maybe because we had drank too much). So we drove for one hour, and then we saw a sign that said "Ohio." We turned around and started in the other direction, knowing that we had been going the wrong way. After we turned around, we decided to stop at the first restaurant. It had been a long day and a long drive, and everyone was starving.

When we stopped at a little hick-town restaurant, no one wanted to go in and get the food. After we argued for a few minutes, one of the girls decided to go in and order the food. We ate in the car and listened to the radio for a while. I was tired of driving, so J.B. drove back to Chicago.

When we got back, it was almost daylight. After we dropped the girls off, we went to the hotel to get some sleep. We didn't sleep long because I had to start work that Monday morning. We got up at 1:00

p.m. Sunday, took a shower, and dressed. We went to get something to eat downtown and then walked around. We took a ride on the subway. It was beautiful. I had never ridden one before. I sat in the subway car and thought how unique it was to be riding underground.

While we were riding, all of a sudden, I looked up in the front and saw that we were coming to daylight. When we reached the daylight, we were going up. I asked Robert what was going on, and he laughed at me and said that the subway turns into a skyway when it leaves the downtown area.

When we got back to the downtown area, we walked to a tall, round building. I don't remember the name of it, but there were two of them just alike, side by side. The buildings had a certain section inside for tours. The tourists had to pay fifty cents to ride the elevator to the top floor, and when you reached the top and got off, there were all sorts of souvenirs. We saw an exit going out onto the roof. There were people out there walking around, looking at the city and taking pictures. We went out there to look too. It was pretty windy outside, probably because we were about twenty-five stories up on the roof. There was an iron railing all around the roof, so you could walk to the edge and look almost straight down. We looked at the whole city and then went back inside. We left the building and went back to the hotel to pack our clothes and checked out. When we left the hotel, we went to the projects to say goodbye to our aunt, and then we stopped at the building where we had dropped the girls off. They invited us in for some whiskey, so we drank and partied a little. Before we knew it, it was twelve-thirty. I had forgotten that I had to start work that Monday morning. I reminded Robert and J.B. that we had to leave. We told the girls that we would be coming back before the summer was over and said goodbye.

It was a long journey home. We had to drive carefully, knowing we weren't in the right shape to try and rush. It was dark outside until we got to Ypsilanti. We could see that the sun would be coming up soon, because it was getting brighter in the east. I knew that I wouldn't have time to take J.B. and Robert home and then get to work, so we drove to J.B.'s house first and dropped him off, and then Robert drove me to work and took my car to his house. When I got off work, he was outside waiting for me. On the way home from work, I was so exhausted that I fell asleep.

Chapter 6

During my adventures with J.B., I went to one of those spur-of-the- moment parties at River Rouge Park in June 1966. While we were there with a group of his friends, J.B. and a friend began to argue over J.B.'s ex- girlfriend. I rushed to break it up, but before I could, they were punching each other. It was pretty dark outside, and we couldn't see anyone very clearly. As I tried to break it up, the guy started fighting with me. When his friends saw what was going on, they ran over and started swinging at me. I grabbed the fellow that J.B. was fighting with and wrestled him to the ground. I pulled out my pocketknife and told his friends to get back. Before I knew it, he jumped from the ground right into the knife, believe it or not. Everyone got quiet, and J.B. and I ran to my car and drove back to Ecorse.

J.B. knew they would come looking for him because they didn't know me, so he went home and got a .22 pistol. We went to the main street in Ecorse and waited for them—and sure enough they came, with two full cars. When they all got out of the cars, I didn't know if I should run. I was so confused, so I just shoved my hand in my pocket where the knife was, waiting to see what was going to happen. J.B. and I stood beside each other. They would have surrounded us if it hadn't been for a store behind us. I didn't know any of the group. They had axes, baseball bats, sticks, etc. One guy walked directly in front of us and asked J.B., "Where is your cousin?" While he was talking, he was looking straight at me. He took a swing at me. J.B. jumped in the way and got knocked to the ground. I pulled my knife and stuck the one that knocked J.B. down, and then they all started in the fracas. The one with the axe raised it to hit me from the side, and J.B. shot him in the stomach. When the rest of them heard the shot, they ran everywhere, trying to get away.

J.B. and I went to Hamtramck and got some of my friends, and when we returned, the police were waiting for us. They put everyone who was in my car in jail, and the next morning the detectives took us out, one by one. I was the second to go. I thought I had learned my lesson about fighting, until I was put in jail after the fight in Ecorse. What had happened to me was a foolish mistake. The way I felt in jail was terrible. I couldn't sleep at all. I thought they were going to keep me in jail for the rest of my life. I prayed that if I got out of jail that time, I would never go back again.

When I went into the detective's room, I didn't hesitate. I told them everything that happened. I didn't know what they were going to do. I thought they were going to give us a beating and everything you could imagine, but they treated us with respect. They told us that the two guys that were cut were okay, and the one that was shot was doing all right. I felt so relieved.

After they gave us a thorough investigation, the police let us go. I was shocked. I had expected them to let my friends go but not J.B. and me. On my way home I didn't have the courage to tell my mother. I knew how she would react, and that would hurt me even more. When we arrived at my house, my mother was sitting on the front porch, reading the paper. When I approached her, I could tell by her expression that she knew something was wrong. When I told her, she wanted to cry, but she held it back. She said, "When are you going to learn? I just don't know what to say."

The next week I received a phone call from a detective, asking me to report to his office after work. When I reported, they locked me up. They let me make a phone call, and I called my mother and she got me a lawyer. I got out of jail that next day, and I missed that workday. I continued going to work, but I didn't tell anyone at work what had happened. I thought I would lose my job if the company found out about the trouble I was in.

I received my induction papers from Uncle Sam a month later, after preparing myself mentally to go to court. While I was going to court, my lawyer told me that if I was sentenced or put on probation, I would not be eligible for the army. The state wouldn't let me go anywhere until my case was closed. The charges were dropped on the first account. During this time of going to court almost once a week, I decided to take military leave from Ford, because I was missing too many days of work. After I had taken my military leave, I was out of work for almost two months, without a paycheck coming in. My lawyer told me that if I didn't go to jail, I would be inducted into the army right after my last court case. I was very confused. I didn't know whether to go back to Ford or just find another job until I got the court results. I finally decided to find another job temporarily to help pay bills and the lawyer. I didn't want to go back to Ford; I thought that if they found out what was happening, I would lose my apprenticeship. Since I was on military leave from Ford, I had nothing to lose.

That temporary job turned out to be permanent. While I was working at Champion Spark Plug, my lawyer wrapped up my case, and I didn't have to go to jail or the army. I was placed on probation. I had been working at Champion Spark Plug for over six months before my case was closed. I went back to Ford, but they wouldn't hire me back because I didn't have military papers. So that is how I ended up at Champion permanently.

My first job at Champion was a sweeper and cleaner's job. I had to stay on that job for the first thirty working days; that was my probationary period. After that, I bid on a handyman job, doing odds and ends. I was on the handyman job in department 18 for a little over a year before I was able to get one of the higher-paying jobs a union employee could get, and that was a machine setup and repair job in department 17. It was very rare for a union employee to get a machine setup and repair classification with only a little over a year's seniority. I was very fortunate, and the people who I worked with repeatedly reminded me of that fact.

I mastered the job after a couple of weeks. Within two months my department ran out of material, so my job was completed temporarily. Since there wasn't anything left for me to do, my foreman had to lend me out to the other departments that needed help. I didn't like that idea because nobody wanted to do most of the jobs that needed help. I was stuck. There was an advantage to my being loaned out because I had a chance to discover better opportunities. That's when I became acquainted with department 14. After I had been used for almost three months, I bid on the machine setup and wheel dresser job in department 14. It paid a dime more than my previous mechanic job

Chapter 7

On June 4, 1967, I went with a friend to Canada to explore Windsor. While we were riding around, we spotted a girl walking down the street. We pulled over to the side of the road and asked her where she was going. She said, "Nowhere."

My friend started rapping to her, and I interrupted and said, "Do you have a friend?" and "Do you think I could meet her?"

She said, "I don't know, but I'll call and see if she can come over to my house."

She made arrangements over the phone so that my friend and I could go over to her friend's house and pick her friend up. When she came out of the house, I saw her first. Right then I knew she would be sitting in the back with me. I jumped out of the car and directed her in the back seat. We introduced ourselves. I told her my name, and she said her name was Valerie.

We went to a teenage club in Windsor for a couple of hours and then went to a drive-in restaurant. I smelled baby powder on her, but I didn't think anything of it. On our way back to take the girls home, I asked Valerie if I could see her the next day, which happened to be a Sunday. She said, "I don't know. I have a daughter, and I don't know if I can get a babysitter." Tina Marie Porter was born on April 26, 1967.

I said, "Can you bring the baby?"

She said, "Call tomorrow, and I'll let you know."

We took the other young lady home and headed for home ourselves.

That was the beginning of my romance with Valerie. Our courtship lasted until September 9, 1967, the day we got married. Our wedding was held in my mother-in-law's house on September 9, 1967, in Windsor, Canada. J.B. was my best man, and my wife's cousin, Karla, was the maid of honor. The wedding ceremony was supposed to have been for the immediate family, since the house could only accommodate so many, but more relatives came and were welcomed just the same. It seemed like the hottest day of the year. In fact, it was so hot that my wife fainted right after our ceremonial kiss. She recovered a couple minutes after.

Carl Hubbard and Robert Wilson were both in the military service at the time of my wedding and stationed overseas; Robert was in Germany and Carl in Korea. I missed their being at my wedding.

On November 25, 1968, my daughter Tammy Lynn Lake was born. My father and I became acquainted again. I would take my family over to his house about once every other month. Since I was much older and more mature, I began to understand his ways and his point of view on life. I found out that he only had an eighth-grade education, and after he left that grade, he had to make a living for himself and help his family out. He was born in Alabama, and there weren't very many things a black man could do in those days to make a living, but he managed to survive. He had always been a very independent person. His philosophy was "If I can make it, anybody can."

In May 1971, my father's second wife Dorothy died of a heart attack. She was only forty-two at the time of her death. They say that the good die young. If you had met her, you would truly believe that statement.

About a year later, my father remarried again. This time he married a woman with a twelve-year-old son. Her name is Cora, and her son's name is Carl. She is a very warmhearted person. That is one thing about my father: he always marries a person with a beautiful personality.

My maternal grandmother died when I was a very young boy. I don't recall having any memories of her. I remember my maternal grandfather only slightly; after my grandmother died, he very seldom came around. The last time I saw him was in 1965.

My maternal great-grandparents lived downstairs from where I was born. We were very close. When my mother got her first job, my sister, brother, and I spent most of our time downstairs. My great-grandfather was a card player; he loved playing cards. He taught me how to play cards at a young age. In fact, I had begun to play cards so well that I beat him in a game of cards one day, and he whipped me with his cane because he said I was cheating (but I wasn't). I remember how my great- grandmother would take me shopping with her. We would walk, and it took about a half an hour to get to the shopping area. She died in 1957, and four years later my great-grandfather died.

I never did get a chance to meet my paternal grandparents because they lived in Alabama and never came up north. My paternal grandfather died before I was born, and my paternal grandmother died in the younger years of my life.

My wife's maternal grandparents are two of the most beautiful people I have ever met. They make me feel like they are my original grandparents. I can't express in words what they mean to me.

My wife came from a large family. There are eleven children, five boys and six girls. The oldest boy is Louis, followed by Wayne, Kevin, Dana, and Michael. The oldest girl is my wife Valerie, followed by Roxanne, Alanna, Pamela, Sylvia, and Bridgette. On May 9, 1963, her father was struck and killed by lightning, while he was fishing in the Detroit River. The death of my wife's father took a lot away from the family, but the unity he developed in the family held them together.

I really enjoy going over to Windsor. The atmosphere is very friendly and warm—not only in my wife's family but in the whole city. I feel a secure sense of awareness. I'm never worried about someone trying to take something away from me, my life, or my worldly possessions.

On January 1, 1970, my mother-in-law remarried. Her husband's name is John Richardson. He had eight children. Only four of them were living with him at the time of their marriage. They were John (known as Buster), Andre, Tony, and Lisa; they were still very young at that time of marriage. The older four were out on their own. With four of my mother-in-law's sons on their own, plus my wife, there was a total of ten children remaining in the household.

During the first couple of months of marriage, it seemed as though I had been given a new life. Everything was going beautifully, until I started spending some of my weekends with my so-called friends. We would go to the bars and sit around and drink, and when we didn't want to go to any bars, we would sit in one of our cars and ride around the city, drinking and talking about old times.

This went on for three or four months until my wife got fed up with my leaving her home on the weekends. She told me that I was spending more time with my friends than with family. I could see in her eyes that she was very upset with my going and leaving her home most of the time. I just didn't like the way she was telling me how to spend my time. We argued about it for a few minutes, until

I got mad, and then I decided to leave the house for a little while. I got into my car and drove away. As I was driving through the city, I thought about the argument. I began to see how right my wife was. I could see that I had married her to change my life and that I was beginning to fall back into the same old ways again, sitting around wasting my time and money with some of my so-called friends. As I drove, I realized my mistakes and wanted a chance to make up for them. I saw how some of my friends and so- called friends had gotten divorces because of the same mistakes. That was the last thing in the world that I wanted. I decided to go back home and take what was coming to me.

When I got back home, I noticed that my wife had been crying. Hurting the feelings of the person I loved the most made me feel like a rat. Well, we got it back together, and I realized then that nothing could pull me away again.

Chapter 8

When I started in department 14, I had a feeling of responsibility. I went into the department objectively, knowing that I was going to qualify for the job. I didn't have any other choice. There was a black brother named Sam who came to the department about a week before I did. We were the first black men to ever get that job in department 14. It was a hell of a challenge. We had to fight a mental battle with the foreman and some of the workers. The foreman was from the old way of thinking. He didn't believe in social change. He honestly felt that a black man couldn't do the job of a machine setup and repair and wheel dresser. He didn't give brother Sam or me any encouraging words. He told us that he wasn't going to follow us around the shop and that we had better do our jobs. He didn't even explain to us what had to be done or how to do it. The job was very tedious. You had to get about five or six industrial diamonds from the foreman, and then you had to get a long steel rod, about 5/8-inch diameter, and cut it in pieces about 10 inches long. Next you cut a cross in the middle of the steel at one end, down about a half an inch, and then you would file the round end that you had cut the cross on to a point. When you got it filed down to where it looked like four prongs, you would take the best end of your diamond and insert the opposite end into your steel diamond holder. After that you would brace your diamond in the holder and file the brassing off the top, until you could see your diamond's top half. When you saw what shape you had, knowing beforehand what it looked like, then you would decide which side of the diamond you would lay on the lapper, a wheel that revolved in a circle. It had a flat surface that you would put diamond dust on. This diamond dust would cut the diamond down to a certain shape in about one to six months, depending on the hardness of the diamond.

When you really got your diamonds together to perform a decent job, if you didn't have someone else's diamonds to do the job with, it was a possibility that you wouldn't qualify for the job. The reason I'm saying this is because you only had ninety days to qualify on the job. When you start off, it takes you two or three weeks to find out what is really going on. In the next three to five weeks, you may have qualified to set the whole machine up, but you haven't even started your diamond work yet. Learning how to work with your diamond is the major step on the job. This takes anywhere from two months to a year or more. I'm not exaggerating; there are some guys who have been on the job for five to fifteen years and still don't know how to do the job properly.

I had a natural talent for the job. I caught on quickly, knowing that if I didn't, I probably wouldn't have had a second chance. My ego eventually became strong. I kept telling myself that one day I would be the best wheel dresser my company ever had.

When I was qualified, I had only been in the department two and a half months. In order to determine if a man qualified for the job, the foreman would take one of the worker's diamonds and cut a groove into the wheel, about twenty- to forty-thousandths of an inch. The worker then had to take care of nine machines plus redress or put the wheel with the groove in it back in shape. That is what my foreman did to me. I redressed the wheel and gave the sample to the foreman before the day was over. He wasn't too happy, knowing what I had done. He didn't even tell me that I was qualified. All he said was "okay" when I handed him the plug. His attitude made me feel bad, but I kept my feelings to myself; I knew one day he would appreciate my work.

Once I was qualified, there were three other mechanics who qualified as well. We all started on the job around the same time. Sam started a week before me, and my old school buddy Robert Kinsman started a week after I did. Sam went on the afternoon shift because he had bid on that shift when he got the job. He got his training on the day shift. Jeff, Robert, and I remained on the first shift. My company had never had four men training in this department at one time. I found out later that two other men were put on the job a month before we came. In the past you needed about fifteen years' seniority to get this job. The reason for the big replacement was that my company was in the process of moving to a new plant. It had also started an upgrading program for the nonskilled workers who bid off their jobs to help the skill trades to get ready for the big move. These jobs, which were classified as Journeymen's Helper, paid a higher rate than any union job in the shop. In turn, this took the men with the highest seniority off their present jobs temporarily and gave the men with the ability to pass the test a chance to get a higher-paying job.

I was on the job longer than I had expected to be, knowing that it was temporary. I began to master the job. My foreman knew it, but he still didn't have respect for me. I couldn't, or shall I say, I didn't want to believe that he was prejudiced against me, but my diagnosis told me it was so. There were a lot of black women in the shop, who had told me about the foreman's attitude before and after I went to the department. The black women and some of the white women were really thrilled over the fact that I was a mechanic in their department. When I came, it gave them a feeling that things were getting better. I knew by their actions and the way they talked to me that it was my job to set an example for the other black brothers who would follow.

Because I was a qualified mechanic, I had a chance to work overtime on my job when one of the mechanics from the second shift didn't come in. I was second from the bottom on the overtime list, and if someone from the other shift didn't come in, I had to wait until it was my turn to be asked to work. There were eleven men with more seniority, and only seven of them would work every time they were asked. When my turn came, I never refused to work. Some of the older guys didn't like it when I worked overtime, but I didn't care. I was there to make money, just like everyone else. At the end of the week when I got a check with overtime on it, it made me feel as though I wouldn't mind working overtime every day. The job became very easy, and I had plenty of time to myself.

When the big move started, the whole plant was in suspense. Everyone's imagination was running wild. We knew where the plant was located, but we couldn't imagine how it would look inside. When they got a few of the machines set up, they started asking some of the employees to transfer to the new plant. The ones who lived in the neighborhood near the new plant were the ones who wanted to go, knowing it could cut down on their traveling time. There were a few people who lived closer to the new plant than to the old one who didn't want to go to the plant; they wanted to wait until someone else went first.

After my company got all their machines, equipment, people, etc., at the new plant, the company sold the old plant to an adjacent company. When we moved to the new plant, my foreman was promoted to general foreman. During this time, I bought a house that was only a five-minute drive away from the plant. I had managed to save enough money to make a down payment and furnish the complete house. A lot of things changed at the new plant as the move was under way—which caused a lot of problems. My company had to hire new help because of the expansion. These new people weren't in the union, and my company took advantage of their labor. As a result of the new people, the union employees' workload was increased, and the union didn't have a leg to stand on.

There was a problem in department 14 with which I became very familiar. My classification was machine setup and repair and wheel dresser, until we started moving to the new plant. The company changed the classification to machine setup and repair. They dropped the "wheel dresser" part of the classification for a good reason. It was the most important part of the job. The company didn't want to pay for the skilled part of that title. You had to use your diamonds on the wheel to cut one- to three-thousandths of an inch off the wheel without destroying the shape. This part of the job had to be done in order to keep the wheel sharp, so the wheel would keep the machine in production— that is, with a sharp wheel, the material would cut and not break or pop into the operator's face. If an operator on a group of machines had a fairly decent mechanic, one who would take an interest in his work, she would have a fairly decent workday. But if the mechanic didn't have an interest in his job, the operator and the mechanic would start arguing about petty things. For instance, when the mechanic went to fix a machine and he felt that the wheel was sharp enough, he would take his diamonds and just try scratching the wheel instead of cutting it. Well, the operator would go back to work, thinking that she would be able to work the job the rest of the day without any problems, but the same problems would occur again. This time when the operator would go and get the mechanic, he would get a little angry, thinking that the woman just wanted to take time off the machine. If the mechanic had a bad temperament and couldn't control his emotions, he would tell the operator in a sarcastic way, "Take a spare." His attitude would aggravate the operator, and sometimes, depending on the certain operators, this would cause an argument.

Another problem could have occurred when the inspector checked the shape of the wheel in the morning. She asked the mechanic to correct the shapes of the machines that were almost out of tolerance. She wouldn't shut the machine down, thinking that the mechanic would correct the mistake. However, the mechanic wouldn't correct the mistake, and when the inspector checked the shape and saw that it was the same or worse, she would be aggravated. The inspector would tell the mechanic that he had to shut the machine down because it had to be fixed. This would aggravate the mechanic, and he would tell the inspector, "You should have shut it down at the beginning of the shift." This made all the people involved miserable.

These sorts of problems got out of hand when the company dropped the classification of "wheel dresser" from the original classification. [classifications have different monetary values to them.] There was a trick to it, because they only changed the title. We were still doing the same job. I had heard that the mechanics in department 14 were trying to get a raise because they were doing a semiskilled job. They were turned down, and nothing else was said for a long time. This happened about ten years before I came on the job.

Now that my company was aware of some of the major problems, they were spending tens of thousands of dollars trying to perfect a system that would eliminate the process of the mechanic cutting the wheel to keep its shape. They were not getting cooperation from the union employees, and some of the salaried employees were slowing down the new system.

I had been waiting for my company to post a notice when they were going to give tests to union employees who wanted to apply for the apprenticeship program. I had just missed the first apprenticeship program by a month. Usually, they accepted applications for testing the union employees every four years. This time I was waiting for the notice. When the notice appeared on the bulletin board, I was on the midnight shift. I knew that if I got the job, I would be on the day shift for at least four years as an apprentice. I prepared myself mentally, thinking, *I know I'm going to pass this test.*

The day of the test, there were about twenty men in the room. It wasn't a very hard test. In fact, it was the same type of test that I had taken to become a mechanic at my company. I went right through the test and had time to go over it. There were only three questions in the mechanical ability portion that I wasn't sure of. I had confidence in everything else, knowing that I was doing the right thing. I was the first one to hand the test back.

The next day, everyone who took the test was rapping with each other, talking and asking about what answers and questions. Some of the guys asked me a few questions about their answers. They knew I had taken the test, and they felt that I could relieve their minds on some of the things that were puzzling them. Most of them had the same two or three questions that I had. We talked about it, and that was that. I felt inspired knowing some of the guys came to me for help. A few weeks went by, and all the guys who took the test became impatient waiting for the results. We felt we should have heard our scores. A couple of us got together and asked one of the bargaining committee members to find out what was taking the company so long. He went into the office to ask one of the men who was on the apprenticeship committee what the scores were. He told us that he had seen a list on the desk, and then he told me the names of those who had passed, including me. This took the pressure off my mind, knowing I had passed the test. Now all I had to do was wait for an interview. I felt so good that I told some other people at work, and when I got home, I told my wife. That night I went to the store and got a bottle of wine, and the wife and I celebrated.

I had that sensational feeling until a few weeks passed and I wasn't notified for an interview. The committee man had told me I passed the test, so I decided to go and see him. However, he didn't say anything beneficial to me. I went to the chief steward and told him what had happened, and he said he would look into the matter.

Two days later the chief steward came over to my department with one of the men on the apprenticeship committee, and the man on the apprenticeship committee told me that I got 74 percent on the test. He added, "You need 70 percent to pass the test and 75 percent to get an interview; you missed the interview by 1 percent." I still didn't believe I only got 74 percent, so later the same day I asked the chief steward to see if they had the score on my test.

He said, "I will try to do whatever I can, but I'm not allowed to look at the test." I went home that day very puzzled, thinking maybe I should drop the whole matter. But then I said to myself, *What the hell! I believe in myself, and with my past experience, there isn't a doubt in my mind.* I knew I did better than they said I did.

When I went into the house, my kids were waiting for me as usual. I picked them up at the bottom of the stairs at the side door and carried them both to the top. I took my jacket off and stood there for a minute, thinking about what had happened at work that day. My wife came into the kitchen and saw the expression on my face. "What's wrong?" she said.

"Nothing," I said. She knew there was something on my mind that I didn't want to talk about. Later, while we were in bed, I explained to her what I thought was happening.

She said, "Don't worry about it; get some sleep." I kissed her and then went to sleep.

The next day at work, the chief steward came to me and told me that he had talked to the apprenticeship committee. They had agreed to talk with me and explain why I only got 74 percent on the tests.

The next week, the apprenticeship committee called the foreman and told him to send me up front to one of the committeemen's offices. When I got there, all four of the men on the committee were sitting in the room, facing the door. I opened the door and went in, and they told me to have a seat. There was only one empty seat in the room, so I sat in it. I looked at all four men in the room, and I felt that they all had funny looks on their faces. They couldn't look me in the eyes. One of them said, "You passed the tests, but you didn't get enough for an interview." Another one said, "You scored low in mechanical ability and math." The one who told me I scored low in math and mechanical ability was looking at some records on the desk. Another one asked me what I would like to do in the future.

I said, "I would like to get into the apprenticeship at my company and then go from there." One of them said he was sorry, but after all the guys get into the apprenticeship and graduate, they would consider the people who scored 74 percent to 70 percent. I knew that it would take forever before I could get into the program. There were about thirteen guys who had a score that was 75 percent or better, and the committee was accepting only nine apprentices. It would take four years before the nine would graduate, and then the committee would pick the next top nine, etc.

I walked out of the room a little disgusted, knowing that when I was in grade school I was the smartest student in my math classes. Even in junior high and high school, if I wasn't the smartest in the class, I was next. I had always been told that I was good in mechanical ability and math.

Well, I went on back to the department, knowing something wasn't right. I knew that I would have to find out more about those apprenticeship tests, but this time it would have to be in secret, or I would have to bring the NAACP in to investigate. I wasn't going to rush things. I would just take my time and get evidence. There were too many things in my favor proving to me that I had good qualifications in every field.

The next day at work, I sat around talking about anything people wanted to talk about. Most of the people talked about the conditions in the plant. Some of the people spoke about the things that were happening in the world, how bad things were for the poor people. Sometimes there would be about seven or eight guys standing around on our break, rapping face to face, black to white, about the history of the world and the part that man played.

When I saw this one white brother, I knew that he was from a totally different environment from me, and if we both expressed our different points of view, we could obtain some type of understanding. We didn't pull any punches. I told him that the white race as a whole had been the most violent race of people in the history of the world. Right away he had a complex. He asked me what I meant. I told him, "Look as far back into history as you possibly can. The pharaohs came to Africa and put some of the Africans in slavery to build pyramids that were pointing at certain planets at a certain time of the year. Hundreds of thousands of slaves were destroyed because of the pharaohs' egos. They were trying to build a stairway to another planet. It took over a hundred years for the construction of the pyramids, and during that time, there were many pharaohs in control of the construction. As time passed on, many of the pharaohs' people and even some of the pharaohs themselves started losing faith in their plans, believing that God put them on planet Earth because of their sins. Even the Bible tells how man tried to build a tower to reach God, but it was destroyed, and all the people who were on it fell down; when they hit the ground, they were all talking a different language. The people really didn't fall down, but when they found out that they couldn't reach these planets, when they came down, they had different beliefs.

"When Moses came, he led the slaves to freedom from the pharaohs' control. The pharaohs couldn't do the job themselves, so some of them went to Jerusalem and established themselves there. They corrupted the people's minds and almost put them into slavery, but then they tried a different approach. They took control of the land and put a tax on the people. If the people didn't pay, the pharaohs, or maybe we'll call them kings, sent armies out to punish the people. Jesus Christ came and almost saved the people from being crucified by the king's army, but he got crucified himself for trying to make it a better world. The king's royal people split up and went different ways, but they kept their ideas. When a certain king was in Rome, and he built his empire to the point where the people thought he was a god, he wanted to take over the world. He sent his armies out to destroy some of his neighboring kingdoms. When the Roman Empire failed, a lot of the people moved westward to build other empires. Some of the people moved to Russia, hoping that some of the invading armies wouldn't come up that far into the cold regions. "France was the next strongest empire, but it didn't last long. The French system misused the poor people. They practically starved poor people to death until the people overthrew the government. While that was happening, some people left France and went to England to start over. England then became the world power. England became so powerful and had colonized so much land on planet Earth that they came out with a slogan: 'The sun will never set on the English Empire.' This empire lasted for a long time.

"European explorers set out on ships to find new land and riches. These explorers were poor people taking a chance on looking for something they didn't even know existed. Some of the people believed that the world was flat, and if you went too far out in the ocean, you would fall off the world. But that didn't stop them. They traveled so far west until they had discovered America, a new world, as they said. When they landed, they were very surprised when they saw the Indian people. The Indians were friendly. They accepted the white man; they even let the white man come and live on their land with them. When the explorers went back to Europe, they brought with them goods, fur, riches, etc., and told the king and queen about the conditions in America and how beautiful it was. The poor people were fed up with the European system. They were willing to take a chance on going to America and starting a new life. England provided the poor people ships to make the trip but was expecting something back in return. When the poor people from England got to America, they settled down and started building their own government. They bought a lot of the land from the Indians and started cultivating the land. During this construction period, some of the unsolved mysteries of the past were being looked into by the explorers.

"When the explorers got to the continent of Africa, the African people accepted them just like brothers. The Africans fed them, taught them their culture. This lasted for a while, until the wise white man got the idea to take a shipload of Africans back to America to integrate them into their religion. When they got back to America with the Africans, the bad white men had a different idea. They couldn't get the Indians to do their work for them, because the Indians had a strong belief in themselves; they would work only for themselves. They brought back millions of black people to America to be slaves, to cultivate the land and take care of the rich white man's house and kids. When some of those kids grew up, they had deep feelings for the black man. They sympathized with the black man. They even helped some of them escape to freedom, but America still had its problems.

"When the poor people became settled, the English government sent its army over to America to collect taxes from the people. The taxes got heavy. The people got depressed and decided to run the English army out of America. This was war. The poor people of America won. They formed thirteen states and called themselves the United States of America. They drew up a constitution that would benefit all the people in the country, even some of the black people who were free. Things were looking good until some of the people got greedy for money and power. It seemed as though the beautiful American system was beginning to get corrupted.

"The United States had a civil war, North against South, whites against whites. At this time, the South still had most of the black people from Africa in slavery. Some of the black people had escaped to the North, where the white people weren't too hard on the blacks, and some of the black people went to Canada to escape the white man's savage treatment.

"The war between the North and South got very bad. The North started losing the war. When the North realized this, they took a lot of the black people out of the jails and told them that they would have to fight against the South if they wanted their freedom. The black men joined the Northern army to help win the war between the North and South. Some of the laws were changed to show the nation that the black man was a free man, but the South never forgave the North and took its feelings out on the Southern black man. This caused more black people to migrate

North to look for a better living. A very few black people, considering the number that were here, went back to Africa after they got their freedom. The blacks who didn't have any money had to live with other black families.

"When the industries started expanding, the black people got jobs and started to buy their own property. They organized into different groups and started building their own communities. The black people were increasing too fast, so the white man brought poor white people from other countries to the United States to increase the white population. They even brought other races and creeds of people to the United States. That caused more problems. There were people who couldn't get a job, so they had to get aid from the government, and this caused poverty. People had too much idle time. They didn't have anything to do but sit around and think of a way to get money. This caused the people to steal, rob, kill, etc. The government had to increase its police force to combat this uprise in crime. This didn't stop the situation, since some of the police were corrupt.

"America had many problems within, and it looked as though the American dream was coming to an end. And then there was a world war. This helped solve some of the problems in the country. It increased the military and created more jobs for the people. When the war was over, the problem came back. There was more unemployment, and stealing, robbing, and killing increased."

I paused for a moment and the white brother asked me how I knew all this had happened. I told him, "I went to a mixed school —all races, creeds, and colors—where the school system taught me world history and American history. And if what I'm saying isn't true, they better change the history books and send everybody who went to my school, back to school. Now some of the things I told you were my own conclusions of my history lessons. I believe the white race came from another planet, and I believe that man in general came from another planet. But I believe the black man was put here first, and then the Chinese and Indians, because the black man had the best land, climate, natural resources, and food already there at his disposal. I don't believe in evolution, that man came from ape, forming into the physical features that he has now. If he did, man would have seen some type of ape changing into a man from the time man existed until this present day. And I don't believe that God took some dirt from planet Earth and made man.

"I do believe in a Supreme Being and in a very advanced, intelligent black race, because when the black men were put here on this planet Earth, there had to have been some type of intelligent being to have brought them here and put them in Africa, where maybe one day they would be puzzled and believe that they came from the ape family.

"Africa probably is the only natural place in the world where a human baby could survive without the care of a mother. When the white man came to this earth, he didn't have any land of his own because he was brought to Africa, where the black people were living. Almost everywhere he went, he took someone else's land. These are all facts, and if you don't believe me, try looking in the history books and finding out where the white man was created.

"I don't have anything against the white race. It's usually the rulers that lead the people in the wrong direction. But I'm going to say this, and I know there are a hell of a lot of people who see it the same way that I do: The American system is just as good as any other, but there are people who corrupt and control the system and use it for their own personal benefit. People are people, but it's their environment that influences them into doing the things they do. The black people started off on the wrong foot when they came to this country. They didn't have a chance, but today many of the black people have adapted to the American system and a few are living in heaven."

The white brother looked at me sort of strangely. I knew then that I was getting too deep for him. I told him that I would rap with him later. I couldn't get my point across that day, but I knew there would be other days we would get together and draw something of the "truth."

All that day I felt beautiful. In my conversations with some of the people, I could see that some of them couldn't look into the future and see better days coming. That made me feel bad. But when I talked to the ones who had constructive ideas for the future, I knew there was still a chance to open up the minds of people who didn't really understand life.

Several months later, I was moved to the afternoon shift; one of the mechanics came back on the original job, which was in my classification. There was one too many mechanics on the first shift, and I was the one who had to move. I chose the afternoon shift because I had worked midnights before, and my wife was afraid to stay in the house at night without me. The afternoon shift wasn't bad to work; I just didn't like going to work that time of day because I was on the plant baseball team, and working afternoons interfered with my going to games. We practiced two days a week and played one game a week.

I couldn't afford to take off that one day a week to play ball because I was just barely living as it was.

Things were pretty rough. Most of my friends' wives were working to help their husbands make a decent living. I didn't want my wife to get a job because I always believed a mother's place was at home, taking care of her children until they were old enough to earn their own living. I knew how it was when I was growing up. I didn't really have a father, and my mother had to go to work to support us. Most of the time I was out in the streets, doing whatever I could to pass the day away. All these thoughts were imbedded in my mind, and I felt that when I got married, I wouldn't want my wife to work.

Well, I had to sing a different song. Things got rougher than I thought they would. My wife decided to get a job. I didn't object because I knew the situation, even though I hated the idea. I began to develop a negative outlook on life. I knew that man wasn't created to live that type of life, working almost every day except Sunday, not knowing where his next meal was going to come from. I never saw God once come to help anyone or give them food.

Chapter 9

My wife got a job at a bank, working temporarily. This helped our financial problem for a little while. The job she was doing didn't pay much money, only $2.28 per hour. This caused another problem because we had to find someone who would babysit for our two daughters. Luckily, our babysitter lived across the street. That helped out because we didn't have to cart the kids across town. Our babysitter was an elderly Polish woman. We didn't think twice about whether our children would be properly taken care of.

Things were looking nice. I was on the afternoon shift, and my wife was on days. I didn't have to leave the house until 2:00 p.m., and my wife usually got home at 6:00 p.m., unless she had to work overtime. We only had to pay the sitter for four hours. The sitter gave the girls lunch every day. Sometimes she would serve them dinner, and sometimes, when my wife had to work overtime, the sitter had dinner waiting for my wife.

The sitter had relatives who lived in the northern part of Michigan. Once in a while she would go north to visit them during the middle of the week. One day when she had to go up north, she came over to my house and asked me if she could take my children with her. I didn't hesitate to say yes. I knew my children would be well taken care of. It would be a beautiful experience for them.

The next day, when my children woke up in the morning, they were still excited about their trip up north. They were both telling me at the same time how much fun they had. I could picture in my mind the things they were telling me. I knew that it would be something they would never forget. I felt proud of my daughters. I was so pleased that I sang all the way to work. [

The next day when my daughters woke me up, they were singing a Polish lullaby to me. I was shocked, listening to them sing and not understanding a word. I felt my $20 a week for the sitter was worth it. She wasn't just watching them but also educating them. All that day, my children and I had a beautiful time singing, dancing, and playing, until it was time for me to go to work. My oldest daughter, Tina, asked me, "Daddy, why do you have to go to work? How come you can't stay home with us today, Daddy?" It really made me think. Why did I have to go to work that day or any other day? Was I created to spend most of my life working, not really living the way I wanted to? I was working almost every day, only missing work two or three days a year, and just surviving. Is this what I was created for? I wasn't happy with my job because I was bored with it. I knew I couldn't go any higher without an education in this country. I started thinking about life. I knew that man lived for centuries without working in plants to survive. The Industrial Revolution started only about two hundred years ago. Why did man have to invent factories? We don't need factories to survive.

I daydreamed for a few minutes, and then I came out of it. I told my daughters that I had to go to work to make a living for our family. I told them that I had to pay for food for us to eat, clothes for us to wear, lights for us to see, gas to keep us warm and cook the food that we eat, a house for us to live in, and a car to take us everywhere. I think they might have understood, but if they didn't, they will when they get older. All that day I had thoughts that I had never dreamed of previously. I didn't rap much at work that day; I sat down and thought about how beautiful life could really be and watched the actions of the people who were working and talking.

When I got home that night, I rapped with my wife for two or three hours, telling her about the children's trip and the thoughts I had. She was tired, and I knew she wanted to get some sleep to be ready for work in the morning. We didn't get a chance to see or talk to each other very much during the week because of our different shifts, but we made up for it on the weekends. With the little extra money we had, we began to spend most of our weekends in Canada, partying with my wife's relatives in Windsor. When I worked overtime, we would save that extra money until we had around one hundred dollars, and then we would go farther up in Canada, to Toronto or Hamilton. My wife's brother Louis was living in Hamilton. We would let him know when we were coming up, and when we got there, he would take us all over the city. The next day we would all get together—my wife, her brother, some of his friends, and I—and go to Toronto and party all over the city, day and night. When the money got low, we would go back to Hamilton to get some sleep and then return by that long drive home. Some weekends, her brother and one of his close friends would come back with us to spend a couple of days. Those weekends were beautiful. It took a lot of pressure off our minds, and it made us feel like we were getting something more out of life than just working and trying to survive.

Chapter 10

J. B. and I didn't see each other that much when I was courting my future wife, and after I got married, we only got together about twice a year. Our friendship was still there, but we both knew that times were changing and that it was time for us both to establish our own foundation.

On August 23, 1971, I got a phone call from a friend of mine who was a very close friend of J.B.'s. He said, "Hello, Terry?"

I said, "Yes, this is Terry."

He said, "This is Clyde. I got some bad news for you man: J.B.'s dead. The police found him shot three times in the back of the head, and didn't nobody know who did it." I didn't know what to say. I was speechless, hurt, and angry all at the same time. Clyde and I rapped over the phone for a while, and I told him that I would go to J.B.'s mother's house and find out about the funeral arrangements. After I hung up the phone, I cried, and my wife soothed my mental pain.

The next day I didn't want to go to work, but I knew I had to in order to provide a living for my family. I was in a daze all that day. It took me a couple of weeks to get J.B.'s death out of my mind. There isn't anything you can do for the dead, but there is a hell of a lot you can do for the living, if you can only show them how to enjoy instead of destroy.

On August 28, 1971, I had to go to Ecorse, Michigan, because I was one of the pallbearers at J.B.'s funeral. After I left the cemetery

I went back to the church to be with his family for a half hour, and then I had to rush back home, change clothes, and get ready to stand up at my brother Robert's wedding. The wedding turned out beautiful, but I was a drag. That was one hell of a day for me.

Chapter 11

In the fall of 1972, when the leaves were changing colors, a group of my white friends invited my family and me to go on a camping trip up north. They told me how nice it was up there and about the good times you could have. I thought about my old Boys Scout days and the time my daughters went up north, and I knew it would be a hell of an experience for my family. I could picture all of us together in the woods camping. I told them that I would love to go, but I didn't have camping equipment. One of my white friends said he would let me use his tent because his wife and kids weren't going on this trip. "Okay," I said, and I asked where he would sleep. He said that he could sleep with some of the guys who weren't married.

When that weekend came, my wife had everything packed and ready to go. She had asked a friend named Jessie to go camping with us. Jessie stayed overnight with us and was ready to go in the morning. Some of the guys who were going didn't go to work that Friday. They left that Thursday after work. There was another group that left Friday after work. I was still working on the afternoon shift, so I couldn't leave until Saturday morning. I followed a friend of mine who was working the afternoon shift with me.

When we arrived at the camping spot, most of the people were already there and had their tents set up. It looked as though we were at some beautiful little village in a jungle. A lot of my friends came over to the car to greet us. One of my friends who had told me about the camping spot said, "I didn't think you were ever going to come."

I felt like a free man, breathing all that fresh air. There were no streets, no buildings, no loud noise of factories—nothing to disturb the peace. Directly in front of us, it looked like we were on the edge of a cliff. My wife spotted it too. "Terry, look!" she said. She grabbed my hand, and we both took one of our children's hands and walked over to the edge.

All I could say was, "Wow." It was so beautiful. We were about three hundred feet up on the top of Lumberman's Monument, a mountain in northern Michigan. At the mountain's bottom was the Asobo River, and about six hundred feet in the middle of the river was an island full of beautiful trees. On the top of the mountain, you could almost look straight down to the water. There was nothing but trees and sand. As I stood up there with my family next to me, I felt as though I was in heaven.

After my family and I had taken a good look, we went back to the car to unload the food and clothing we brought. The friend of mine I had followed there, had already begun setting his tent up. I helped him finish setting up, and when we were through, another friend pulled into the campgrounds with the friend who had the tent for me. He got out and took out the tent, and I helped him set it up for my family. When we finished, the inside of the tent looked as though it were big enough for six people to sleep in. We packed our goods inside the tent, and then I went with a few of the guys to get some wood to make a fire. It didn't take long. When we got back, my wife and her friend were sitting at a huge fire in the middle of the campground. My daughters were playing with the other kids. There was music everywhere all night long.

Fifty people were in our group. At night we sat around the big campfire and listened to music and partied. My daughters went to bed about 9:00 p.m., and about 2:00 a.m. most of the people went off to their tents to get some sleep. We went to our tent too, but when we got there, my wife's friend asked if she could sleep in the car. My wife said, "You can sleep in the tent with us; there's enough room."

Her friend said, "That's okay; I'll sleep in the car." There wasn't anything I could say, but I knew she would be safe in the car with the doors locked. Anyway, there were some people in our group who didn't go to sleep at all while we were there.

The next morning, we woke up early. It was very cool outside. I lay in my sleeping bag, thinking about getting up and getting breakfast started. My daughters had gotten up and put their clothes on and were outside playing with their friends. My wife reminded me that I had to go and get some water to wash up with. We had brought only cooking and drinking water. There were a couple of guys who went down to the river to get some water, but I didn't like that idea. There were a few people going to a store about a mile or so away, so I took the whole family and my wife's friend in the car and followed them. There was a washroom across the road directly in front of the store. All of us went to the washroom, and then we went to the store to get a few things.

When we returned, we got our breakfast started. I had to get more branches for the fire so my wife could finish the cooking. On my way back with the branches, I smelled the food in the air. When I got to our area, I saw my wife cooking on a portable stove. One of my friends saw the difficult time she was having with our fire, so he let my wife use his stove. This worked out beautifully. She cooked more than enough food. When we finished ours, there was still a lot left, so I gave it to a few of my friends.

One of my friends had brought a three-wheel motorbike with huge tires. They looked like fat, round car tires. Most of the people were taking turns riding the motorbike. I had never driven one before, but I knew it would be easy to learn. When my turn came, I sat down on the seat, put both feet on the two bars, and put each hand on the handlebars. The brakes were on both handlebars, and the gas was on the right handlebar. I sped down the trail, thrilled and excited from the joy of the ride. When I got back, my wife was standing in the crowd, watching me. She wanted to take a turn too, and she did. And then my daughters wanted to ride. When everyone had had a turn, I got back on the bike and took each of my daughters for a ride. They sat in the middle of my lap, and one at a time, we went speeding through the forest.

A few hours later, my family and my wife's friend and I took a long walk along the edge of the cliff. When we got tired, we sat down and rested amidst all the pretty leaves. We even saw a couple of small boats with people fishing.

After we were there for a half-hour, we went back for dinner, and then it was time for everyone to leave. I took the broken-down tent over to my friend and said, "Thanks a million." We rapped for a while, and then I went back to the car. Everyone was in my car and ready to go except my daughter Tina. She was sitting outside on the ground by my door. She was crying. I asked, "What's wrong, Tina?"

She cried and said, "I don't want to go home. I want to stay here." I told her that we had to go for now, but we would come back. A strange feeling of sadness ran through my body. I knew that I would come back, even if I had to bring my family and camp alone. Tina and I got into the car. We were ready to leave.

The drive home was just as beautiful as the way there—until we came to a traffic jam. It was stop-and-go for an hour. Eventually, we climbed back up to our regular speed. When we got near Detroit, I felt bad. I can't fully explain those feelings, but I'll try to describe them: It seemed as though I was driving toward an unimaginable concentration camp, where people were put to be punished for an unknown reason. In this camp, the people inflicted punishment on each other, and the people who had more materialistic things than the majority had a uniformed armed force to protect them from others who didn't have as much. It wasn't just in my mind. It was in the air. I could see it, I could hear it, and I could feel it when it was my time to pay my dues.

When we got back to our house, after dropping off my wife's friend, we took showers. The girls were so tired that they went to their room to take a nap. My wife and I laid back and listened to some sounds on the radio until the girls awoke. When they woke up, it was almost time for them to go to bed for the night. We ate supper, and after that we were so tired that we decided to go to bed at the same time as the girls. I knew my wife had to get some sleep and get up early to go to work.

We talked about our camping trip all week at work. Halloween was around the corner, and the same group of friends was having a Halloween party. I was invited, and I wanted to take my cousin and his girlfriend with me and my wife. I knew it was a private party, so I asked the host if I could bring a friend. He said yes, so I told my cousin about it. I told him that it was a costume party and that everyone would be incognito.

My wife and I went to rent a costume, but there weren't many left. I found one, but my wife didn't like what she saw, so she ended up going to the party as a mummy. I got a white sheet and cut it up into long strips and wrapped her up from head to foot. She had holes in her eyes, nose, and mouth. I forgot to make holes in her ears. I dressed as George Washington. I had to buy the mask when I rented the costume, so I painted the face black and borrowed one of my sister's wigs. When Robert came to the house, he had a mask that covered his whole face. Robert's girlfriend was dressed as a rabbit, and a friend she had brought along with her had a mask that covered her whole head.

I ended up having more fun at that party than I had ever had in my life.

Chapter 12

That year drifted by with its usual ups and downs. I managed to get back on the first shift before the year was over. That made me feel good because I got a chance to see my wife more. We had a chance to go to the movies during the week and visit our friends in the city, who we didn't ordinarily have a chance to see.

A few weeks before New Year's Eve, I went by Robert's house, and we sat around, talking about some of the good old days. I asked him if he wanted to go to Toronto with my wife and me. He said he would like to, but he wasn't sure because he had broken up with his girlfriend. Two days before New Year's Eve, Robert called me and said he was going. We rapped on the phone about the trip, and I told him that I wasn't going to tell Louie, my brother-in-law, that we were coming. I wanted it to be a surprise.

It had snowed only once or twice near the end of the year. On Friday, New Year's Eve of 1972, I was supposed to pick my wife up at five o'clock from work. She had taken a change of clothes with her to work, so she wouldn't have to return home before we left. Unfortunately, she had to work overtime that day. I sat in the car, waiting impatiently for her. I knew Robert was at home, wondering what was taking us so long. She finally came out at 6:10 p.m. and asked where Robert was.

I said, "He's at home waiting. I didn't pick him up because he said he wouldn't be ready until 5:30 p.m."

When we got to his house, he was sitting on the front porch. He said, "Let's go in my car. I got some new tapes that we can listen to on the way up."

I said, "Okay."

My wife got out of our car and got into Robert's; he helped me put our clothes into his trunk. We were off and running.

It was night when we left. There were a few clouds in the sky. You could see a full moon smiling right in your face. The stars were sparkling very bright, and the weather was beautiful for that time of the year. There was no snow on the ground and very little traffic on the road. Robert drove halfway, and I drove the other half. While we were driving, my wife sat in back and tried to get some rest.

When we drove into Hamilton, it was almost ten o'clock. We decided to go to Louie's place instead of looking for a place to stay. We had only two hours to find Louie, change our clothes, and go to a Hamilton nightclub before it was the New Year. When we got to his place, Louie's landlady told us that he had left for Windsor about five hours earlier. That ended that surprise. There were a few of his friends at the house, who told us where we could go to have a good time. One of them said that we wouldn't need reservations for his suggested club. He said they planned to go and that he would try to save us a table. The landlady told us that we could stay there if we wanted to. We didn't stay, but we changed our clothes there and we went to the club.

There was a small line outside the club. We parked the car and went and stood in line, hoping to get in before midnight. We only had five minutes. Unfortunately, we couldn't get in, and all the other places I knew were full, so we waited. It was about twenty minutes after twelve when we walked into the club. I saw a few people my wife and I knew. There were no seats near them. I then saw the people who were at Louie's place, but there were no seats near them either. We found some empty seats directly in front of the stage, about thirty feet back, on a small platform. It seemed as though everyone in the place was having the time of his or her life. There were about seven or eight black people there, but you wouldn't have noticed it. We had a very enjoyable New

Year's morning, even though we didn't get in until after midnight. After we left the club, we had something to eat, and then I drove the car to Louie's place for Robert to stay there. I drove to a motel and got a room for my wife and I.

Later that day, we went to pick Robert up. When we got there, we found out where a very close friend of Louie's and mine was. We went and found him. After we found him, he picked up a girlfriend and a friend of hers and we went to Niagara Falls. When we got back from the Falls, we dropped the two girls off, and that night we went together to Toronto and partied. We partied in Toronto and Hamilton until it was time to return to Detroit.

The roads were terrible on our way back to Detroit, until we were almost one hundred miles out of Hamilton. It was smooth driving the rest of the way.

I got that same funny feeling as we drove near Detroit, only this time I could see Detroit. My wife was in the back seat asleep. Robert and I had been rapping all the way back to Detroit. When that feeling came on me, I told him how I felt, and he said he felt the same way. There wasn't anything we could do about it. It was as though a suffocating mist engulfed us, leaving our feelings completely drained. We were really prisoners in this so-called free society—temporarily.

We changed the subject. We started talking about school and going to college. I told him that I had decided to go back to college and get some kind of degree. I said, "My wife and I want to have another child, hopefully a boy. When she gets pregnant, she is going to quit work. I know I've got to either work two jobs then or get a better job than what I have. Where I work, they aren't really giving the black man any kind of a good position. I've been out there so long that I know I can run that department by myself, probably the whole shop. They have really been giving me the runaround there. Just because I know my job so well, they try to get me to do things they would not even ask most other guys to do. I feel the other mechanics are making just as much money on the same job that I'm on, and I am not going to break my back doing someone else's job."

"What do you mean doing someone else's job?" he asked.

I explained to him about fixing the wheels that get messed up by other workers. "I can fix any of the wheels they mess up, but most of the guys can't or don't. Why should I fix something someone else messes up, when most of them don't even fix their own?" I said.

Robert said, "Well, you know how that is, and you're black too."

We were going to stop in Windsor to find Louie, but it was late, and we all had to go to work that next day.

About ten days later, I enrolled in Wayne County Community College. I had made up my mind that I was going to get myself a better education. I knew that if I did, I would be able to get a better job and solve some of the problems that I was having and would have. I started school objectively, putting all my small problems aside, everything and everybody except my family, and I got right down into my books. I started by going part-time. I took two classes in data processing. This got me started, giving me a chance to get back in the groove. I programmed all the knowledge I could get from my instructor into my mind. I had a beautiful feeling when I went to class, answering some of the questions the instructor asked. I did very well. In fact, I got an A in both classes.

I knew I was ready then, but I didn't go to school that summer. I had been neglecting my family by going to school and working full-time. I knew that I would be going back in the fall, so I tried spending all my leisure time with my family that summer. School ended in the first part of May, and I had until September to really enjoy my leisure time. My wife was still working. She decided to quit working in September because Tina would be starting school then. We had had our problems with sitters for our girls. When I went back on the day shift, we had to find someone to watch the girls full-time because the Polish woman had too many things to do early in the morning. I asked a friend of my wife to watch the girls, assuring her they wouldn't give her trouble. She agreed to watch them until she found another job. I didn't know anyone who would be able to watch them indefinitely for the price I was able to pay, so I gave her $25 a week. When I worked overtime and my wife had to pick the girls up, I gave the sitter a little extra.

One day at work, while I had been sitting around for three hours, I became very tired and my eyes were about to close. I got up and went for a walk. I went to the men's john; all the toilets were filled, so I sat on the bench and waited my turn. That was the biggest mistake I ever made. I don't know how long I sat there waiting for a toilet, but I closed my eyes, and when I opened them, my general foreman was standing on the side of me. He had probably just come into the john because he didn't have enough time to wake me up or get a witness. He told me to get out of the john, and I said, "I've got to use the toilet."

He said, "I know you're going to say that you weren't sleeping!" I told him that I was waiting for one of the toilets and that I had just closed my eyes, but the only thing he was concerned with was the fact that I had my eyes closed. When he walked out of the john after our conversation, I did what I had to do and went back to my area. About two hours later, my general foreman called me into his office and wrote on my work record that I was caught sleeping. He felt that he was just and I had to suffer the consequences of my mistake.

Before summer was over, we had to find another sitter. This time we found an elderly black woman who lived in my old neighborhood. I gave her twenty-five dollars a week. She watched a friend's child also. My mother took my daughters there every morning and brought them home when she got off work. I had known the woman most of my life, and she took care of our daughters as though they were her own. At home they talked about things they had done, and I believe I was very fortunate to have someone take that much interest in my children.

I got back my income tax returns the last week of school. My wife and I had been talking about buying camping equipment. I felt this was probably the best time to buy some, so we figured out approximately how much money we would be able to spend. Knowing that my wife would be quitting work in September, and that we would need extra money for the camping trips, we had to keep some money on hand in case of an emergency.

My old friend Carl and I went looking for a sale on tents and all other camping equipment. We had been talking about camping at work and were trying to get a group of black friends to go. He knew everything that we would need in the way of equipment from his past experience. That helped out a hell of a lot, because I didn't know much at all. That day we got most of the things that we needed. My wife picked up all the other little things that we couldn't think of.

Baseball season started, and I was debating whether I should play ball that year. I knew that it would take time away from my family if I played. I thought that I would see how my wife felt about my playing ball. When we talked about it, she said, "You know how well you like playing baseball. Why are you asking me?"

I said, "Well, you know we haven't been spending that much time together, and I had told you that we would make it up in the summer. If I play ball, you know I'm gonna have to go practice plus play in the games. Besides, I would then spend a little time with the team after the games."

She said, "Well, that will be something the kids and I enjoy anyway."

I felt good knowing she was in my corner.

Chapter 13

Willie Webster, Carl, and I were rapping one day at work about a skiing trip Webster and friends had gone on in Grayling. My wife and I were supposed to have gone, but we didn't have enough money to take the trip. During the conversation, Carl and I mentioned our plans for a camping trip. Webster told us he had seen some beautiful camping areas in Grayling. There were places where you could rent canoes, which sounded pretty good to us, so we decided to take our families there that following weekend. Before we left Detroit on our 250-mile journey north to Grayling, it started to rain, making our trip a little miserable. However, when we reached our destination, the sky was clear, making our trip worthwhile after all.

Willie led the way and decided to stop to get gas. From there we went directly to the canoe post and inquired about canoes. A white fellow, who was sitting behind a desk, exchanged greetings and asked us if he could be of any assistance.

Willie said, "Yes, we want information about renting canoes."

The young white fellow asked, "How long would you like to rent them? We rent them by the hour and the day. The more canoes you rent, the less you'll have to pay. Here's a map showing our trail and pickup spots." He told us about the current in the river; it was strong in some places and could take us down the river to pick up spots without paddling. It sounded beautiful to us, and we agreed to go back in a couple of weeks and rent canoes for two or three days.

The young white fellow overheard us talking and said, "If you don't want to rent the canoes today, it would be best for you to make reservations for a certain day and tell us what time we should be expecting you to come. We'll have the canoes ready when you get here." He even said if we couldn't get there until late in the afternoon, we could camp on their grounds overnight until we got ready to leave the next day. We made the reservations, but we couldn't decide on how many canoes to rent. We had figured on bringing more people back with us, but we didn't know how many for sure. We knew that the three of us were going to bring our ladies and my girls. Willie said that he thought one of his closer friends would probably come. We decided to ask the young fellow to reserve four canoes. We put Willie's name in the book, and the fellow gave us literature on canoeing and a map of the different camping areas. We went back to the cars. My wife and daughters were outside the car, standing around and looking.

My wife grabbed me by the hands and called the girls over to us. She said, "Tina, Tammy, do you want to go and sit by the water?" She looked at me and said, "Let's go sit over there in the shade by the water." I followed. We sat there for a while, watching some of the people who rented the canoes. It looked very exciting. My imagination got carried away, wondering what was beyond that bend out ahead. We got up and went back to the car.

Willie and Carl were standing near the cars talking. I asked Willie what time it was. He told me. It was still early, and he said, "Do you want to go horseback riding?"

I said, "Yeah, but what about my wife and girls?"

He said, "They have an animal farm across the road from the horse stable. Your wife could take the kids there. It will probably cost them a quarter to get in." I agreed.

We drove over to the stable. It wasn't that far away, about a five-minute drive. It was a very big place, and they had a very large fenced-in place for the horses. My wife left for the animal farm, and Carl, Willie, and I went inside to rent the horses. It cost us three dollars an hour, and if we brought the horses back hot, they said they would charge five dollars extra. Knowing that, we were very careful. In fact, we didn't keep the horses for the hour. I believe we brought them back after half an hour.

When I got off the horse, my wife came over and said, "The kids want to ride those little ponies over there." I asked one of the helpers how much it would cost to rent two small ponies. He told me the price, and I rented two for the girls. Carl walked a horse with Tina on it, and I walked the other with Tammy; my wife and Willie walked with us. Tina and Tammy were thrilled over the ride. When we got back to the stable, we sat down in some chairs and relaxed, watching the girls as they played around. I thought of how beautiful everything was and tried to imagine how nice it would be on our canoe trip.

It was getting late, and we knew we had a long drive ahead, so we got into the cars and headed back home. When I came to that same location where I knew Detroit was near, those same feelings returned, as I imagined Detroit as a controlled concentration camp. When I reached home, the feeling was gone. I didn't go anywhere that night. I stayed home with the family and watched television.

A couple of weeks passed. I played a few baseball games with the plant's ball team. I knew we didn't have the unity we had had in previous years. There was a constant argument going on with our team and dissension among the players. It just didn't seem as though we should have been out there playing. We were making fools of ourselves. At some of those games, I wished I was in the middle of the forest, enjoying nature.

The weekend for our canoe trip arrived. My wife prepared our camping equipment and food Friday night, and when Saturday morning came, we were up bright and early. We packed everything into the car and left our home at 5:45 a.m. for Carl's place, where we were scheduled to meet at six o'clock. My family was the first one there. Willie pulled up with his lady friend, Theresa, about a minute after me. I got out of my car to rap with Willie and asked him who else was coming. He told me that his best friend couldn't make it, and he said he didn't know if anyone else was coming. About three minutes after we started rapping, Carl and his wife, Francis, came out of their apartment and started packing their things into his car. After Carl got everything packed, he asked, "Are you ready?"

I smiled and said, "Yeah."

Carl asked Willie if anyone else was coming, and Willie answered no. We got into our cars, and we were off and running.

We arrived in Grayling, Michigan, at 9:45 a.m. It was a very warm and clear day. We signed in at the canoeing office and had to cancel one canoe because we couldn't get anyone else to go with us. We took all our equipment and food out of the cars and loaded it into the canoes. I had so many things packed into my canoe that I didn't have any room for a cooler, a box of food, and one of my daughters. I asked Carl if he could take the cooler and box of food and asked Willie if he could take Tina. They both said yes. We were off.

The current in the water was stronger than it appeared to be. I got ahead of Carl and Willie and tried to stop the canoe to wait for them. It was almost impossible. I had to guide the canoe ashore and grab a thick, overhanging branch in order to stop the canoe. As I sat there in the canoe, waiting and talking to my wife and daughter, I reminded my wife of the day we came to Grayling to make reservations. We sat under the tree thinking about what it was going to be like then, and now we were there. "Everything is almost the way I pictured it," I said.

I looked around and saw Carl coming on strong, but I didn't see Willie. Willie and Theresa couldn't get their paddling together. Theresa hadn't paddled before, and Willie wasn't used to the current yet. But it didn't take long for Willie to control his canoe; he became so adjusted that he led part of the way.

We canoed about twenty-two miles the first day and stopped only once before we came to the campgrounds for the night. We had been on the water for almost eight hours. It didn't take us long to pitch our tents. The women started preparing the food, while Carl, Willie, and I went to get some firewood. When we got back, we started the fire and cooked the food. It began getting dark outside.

When we finished eating, all of us sat around Willie's campfire and rapped about the good time we were having. We listened to a group of Presbyterian teenagers and their chaperones sing a song around a nearby campfire. It was a beautiful experience out there in the middle of nowhere. We were having a wonderful time with the family, watching a young group of teens, black and white together, who were enjoying nature and having one of the best times of their lives.

Tina and Tammy were getting tired, so I put them in our tent. They changed their clothes, and I tucked them into their sleeping bags and kissed them goodnight. I went back to Willie's fire and snuggled up to my wife under a blanket. It was cool that night. There were no clouds in the sky. You could see thousands of stars. I even spotted one of the planets very clearly when the sun had set. My fire had gone out about twenty minutes after we had finished cooking. Willie's fire was still going because Carl and I had brought our extra firewood over. As it began to die down, we poured water over the fire to put it out, and we all went to our tents for the night.

That next day, early in the morning, Tina and Tammy were up with their clothes on, playing outside. My wife had a hard time waking me up because I had had a fifth of wine in the course of the night. I finally got up when she said she couldn't cook unless I got wood to make a fire. When I came out of the tent, Carl and Willie were already up. Carl said he had gotten up before the sun rose. We went to get wood, so all of us could wash up and cook our breakfast. Willie had brought a portable gas stove that came in very handy. After I ate, I took Tina and Tammy down to the river and watched them as they played in the water. The current wasn't strong there because it was a very wide area and because of a bend in the river.

About twenty minutes later, I took the girls back up to the tent so they could change clothing. I lay down on my sleeping bag to get a little rest. As I began to get situated, my wife came in and lay next to me. When the girls went back outside, my wife and I wrestled around, and then we both fell asleep.

All of a sudden, Willie yelled toward our tent. "Hey, Terry, it looks like it's going to rain! What do you want to do?" I got up and looked outside. The first thing I noticed was both Willie and Carl were taking their tents down. I looked into the sky and saw that a storm was coming.

I yelled back, "What do you want to do? Do you want to try and make it to the pickup spot?"

Willie said, "I think we better try to make it, because it might not stop raining."

Carl had finished taking his tent down, so I went over to help Willie, and then the three of us took mine down. Everyone helped pack the canoes. When we finished packing them, I had room in my canoe to put all my equipment in plus Tina and Tammy. We were off. The clouds were getting darker, and the women were afraid of getting wet. We didn't have any choice but to paddle on. Even though the sky was looking so gray, I still enjoyed looking at the scenery around us.

About four hours after we left the camping spot, I spotted a storefront ahead on the edge of a hill next to the river. My canoe was on the left side of the river, and it just so happened that the store was on the right. The river was at its widest, so I tried paddling as hard as I could to dock where you could pull your canoe up on the left shore. I didn't make it. My wife used her paddle too, something she didn't have to use before. Until then it was easy for me to keep the canoe going at a fairly rapid speed. We did make it to the other side, but it was about thirty yards from the store. I had managed to grab a hold of a long branch that was hanging beyond the water, but in the process, I dropped my paddle into the water and it floated out of sight. I tied the rope from the canoe to that branch and told my wife to hold on until I got back.

Carl and Willie spotted us, and I yelled to them and told them by pointing that there was a store on the hill. They paddled their canoes over to the spot I had missed. I had to struggle through twenty yards of weeds and bushes before I could get to an open area. I eventually reached Carl and Willie. They left their women standing by the canoes, and we went to the store to get some pop, candy, and ice. The store was a cabin made of logs, with a large dining area, a bedroom, and a ten-by-fifteen room used as the store area. A little old lady worked the store and owned the cabin. She was one of the friendliest strangers I've ever met. Carl and Willie got the last three bags of ice left in the store, so she went into her own icebox and pulled out two trays of ice and put it into a plastic bag for me. I was very grateful. When I left the store, Carl and Willie were waiting for me. I told them what had happened, and Carl said, "I'll take you over to your canoe."

Carl and I shoved Willie and Theresa off, and then Francis got into the front of their canoe. I got into the middle, and Carl shoved us off and then jumped in. We headed directly for my canoe. As we got near, I got on my knees to grab a hold of the branch my wife was holding. When I reached out to grab it, the branch and my weight pulled me right out of Carl's canoe, and I splashed into the water. I was lucky I still had hold of that branch. I pulled myself out of the water and into our canoe. I took my wife's paddle, untied the rope from the branch, and we were off again. About a hundred yards down the river, I spotted my other paddle. It was stuck against the bank where the river had a bend in it. This time I was very careful. I reached out very slowly and got the paddle. I took the one that I had, put it in the canoe, and used the other one to carry us onward.

From the spot where I found my paddle, it took us an hour and a half to reach the pickup point. We got there about an hour before the white fellows were scheduled to arrive. The sun was out then; it didn't rain at all. While we were sitting waiting, my wife and daughters took their shoes and socks off and tried to catch some tadpoles with a cup. There were hundreds of them, but my wife and daughters couldn't catch one. Theresa saw what they were doing, and she got a big plastic bag and joined in on the fun. Francis then joined and caught several. Willie stood on the shore and took pictures. We had a lot of fun at that spot, and when the station wagon came to pick us up, we didn't want to go, but we knew we had to.

On the way back to the canoeing office, Tina, Tammy, and I fell asleep in the station wagon. When we got to our cars, I woke up. That was one adventure I would never forget. We got everything packed into the cars and said goodbye to the young white fellows.

It was about four o'clock and the day was still beautiful; the sun was as bright as ever. It was a long and enjoyable ride home—until I came to that old fork in the road. The vibration ran through my body again. This time my thoughts got deeper when I thought how people were being controlled—human beings starving in a big city, with no job or steady income, working like machines all their lives, with nothing to show for it.

We all went our own way when we reached Detroit. When I pulled in front of my house, I unloaded the car and went straight to the shower. After that, I lay down across the bed to recuperate from the long journey home.

Chapter 14

When vacation time came, I didn't have a chance to go anywhere because my wife was working. She had planned to take a week off during my vacation, but she had to take a week of vacation a week before because of an illness. The three weeks I had for vacation went by very fast. During those weeks, I spent most of my time with Tina and Tammy. About twice a week, we would go downtown and pick up my wife and take her out to lunch, usually a little picnic at Belle Isle. I passed a great part of the day away reading books, trying to build up my reading ability. I had read more books that year than I had read in my whole life. In fact, when I graduated from high school, I had only read two books. Reading was something that I had really hated, but now that I understood the purpose of reading, I tried to read whenever I got a chance.

Vacation was over, and I was back at work doing the same old thing, trying to survive. Work was really like a concentration camp. There were no windows in the shop. They only played one type of music, and if there were complaints, the authority would say, "If you don't like this music, we won't play any at all."

You were allowed in certain areas at certain times. You weren't allowed to read at work—that was like committing a sin. They even threatened to fire an employee if they caught him or her reading twice. The job that I had wasn't a production job, and I had plenty of spare time, and my foreman knew it. However, he still wouldn't let me or anyone else read. The union we had at the plant was very weak. Most of the once-a-month meetings that we had were canceled because there weren't enough people to conduct one legally. Many of the people complained about the conditions in the shop, but only a few had enough education to try to do something about it. Unfortunately, they only accomplished a few minor things.

Labor Day was coming up, and my wife and I made plans to go camping that weekend. We wanted to make up for the restricted vacation. When the time came, we were ready. We packed our camping equipment the prior Friday night and were on our way Saturday morning. We headed for Holly, Michigan, to a four-day party, with some of the biggest entertainers in the county, along with rides and entertainment for the kids. On this particular camping trip, I took my family and two of my wife's sisters. It rained all that Saturday, until we reached Holly, when it stopped raining.

I had read in the paper that the affair was going to take place on a VIP's farm. He had almost seventeen acres. Knowing this ahead of time, I figured that I would be able to camp on the VIP's farm. When we got to the VIP's farm, I saw a huge tent directly behind what appeared to be two houses. I turned into a long driveway and drove all the way to the back, where I saw about four people barbecuing spareribs inside the tent. I had expected to see a large group of people partying; I guessed the weather had stopped the people. It looked as though it was going to rain any minute.

I had the car packed with camping equipment and food, and there was just barely enough room for us. My wife and the kids wanted to hurry up and set up the tent, but I told them I would have to ask the owner for permission first. I took it for granted that the VIP would let us camp on his farm because he was black. I got out of the car and went over to a tall black fellow and asked him if he knew where the owner was. He told me that the owner had gone to town and would be back soon. I asked, "Do you know the owner quite well?"

He said, "Yes, he's letting me rent his farm to have this four-day affair."

I said, "Do you think he would care if we camped on his land?" He said, "I think he probably would let you, but you have to ask him because it's not my place." I went back to the car and told my wife that we would have to wait until the owner came.

My wife said, "It's pretty cold out here, and it looks like it's going to rain. Maybe we ought to go and find a motel to stay in tonight. You don't know when he'll be coming in."

I said, "It's still a little light outside. Let's wait until the sun gets ready to set, and if he isn't here, then we can go to the motel we passed or we can find another place to camp around here." She agreed, and she and the kids got out of the car and went walking around the place. There weren't any rides there that I could see. The only thing I saw was an old empty platform.

I got out of the car about five minutes after my wife had left. As I started to walk around, I noticed that one of the houses on the property was actually a bar. I saw a car turn onto the VIP's driveway, headed toward me. For a few seconds, I thought it was the VIP, but by the condition of the car, I realized it couldn't be the VIP. It was six young men. I thought they had probably just come there for entertainment. They drove over to the tent and got out. I walked over to them and started rapping. They told me that they were in the band. One of them said, "We were here last night, but we didn't play because the weather was bad and no one showed up. We'll probably play tonight if the weather doesn't get any worse. Are you from Detroit?"

I said, "Yes. I brought my family up here to camp for the weekend and to see what's going on."

My wife and the girls came back from their walk down by a little lake at the bottom of the slope, near the VIP's house. They came over to the tent where I was, and we watched the band set up their equipment. It got colder outside.

My wife said, "Let's go to that motel down the road to see if they have any vacancies."

I said, "Okay, we can check, and if they do and the VIP says we can't stay, we'll spend the night there. In the morning we'll find camping grounds around here."

We all got into the car, and I drove down the road to the motel. On the way to the motel, I spotted a sign that said, "Camping Site." It was some relief, knowing there was a campground in the area.

I drove into the parking lot of the motel and parked the car. There was a middle-aged woman behind the registration desk in the motel. When she saw me, she looked at me from my head to my feet, staring at the big jungle hat I wore. The first words that came out of her mouth were, "Sorry, we don't have any vacancies."

I went back to the car and returned to the farm. When we got there, I got out of the car and asked the same gentleman if the owner was back. He said, "No. I don't know what's taking him so long. He should have been back by now."

I went back to the car and started it up, so I could turn the heater on for my wife and the kids. We sat there for half an hour. Finally, I saw a 1968 Pontiac convertible turn onto the private drive. The driver went right on up to the bar and parked. I saw the gentleman that I had been talking to approach him, say a few words, and then point to me. The VIP looked at me as I got out of the car and then went into the bar. I walked over to the gentleman and said, "Was that the owner?"

He said, "Yes. He wants you to talk to him later." Frustrated, I walked into the bar and saw the VIP tinkering with a light switch.

I said, "I was asking that gentleman who the owner of this place was, and he told me you are. I wanted to know if I could set my tent up for the weekend on your property. My wife and kids are in the car waiting for me, and it's getting sort of dark. I have to know whether you're going to let me."

He said, "I'm sorry, but I can't; if I let you, other people will want to do the same thing."

I really wanted to set the tent up there, because my stepfather, mother, sisters, brothers, and more relatives were coming to the farm on Sunday. and I wanted to be somewhere near when they showed up. Unfortunately, I had to go back to the car and tell my wife and the kids that we had to leave. We drove back to the area where I saw the camping sign. We followed the arrows that directed us through curved roads, down to the camping area. The camping area was located directly behind the VIP's house. As we drove over to a vacant spot. I heard loud music. Directly below us there was a motorcycle group having a get- together. It looked as though there were about seventy people having the best time of their life. They were playing music, dancing, and singing.

After I had the tent set up, I lit the gas heater and sat it in the middle of the tent. By that time, it was dark, so dark you couldn't see ten feet in front of you. Everyone got back into the car, and we drove back to the VIP's farm. When we reached the driveway, we could hear the music the band was playing. I parked the car, and all of us got out and went over to the tent where the band was playing. There were about fifteen people there. It was very enjoyable sitting inside the tent and listening to the band's music. They were really getting down. During one of the breaks, I went outside and rapped with a couple of the black brothers in the band. One of them said, "I thought you were gone."

I said, "Well, I had to go and find a place to camp." He said, "I thought you were going to camp here."

I said, "You know how some people are when they get a little money. They think they own the world and don't want to be involved with the lower class."

He said, "Yeah, I can tell by the way some of these people are acting."

One of the other black brothers came over to where we were and started rapping with us. About five minutes later, some of the people in the tent were shouting for more music. The three brothers who I was rapping with went back inside the tent to get ready, and I went to sit with my wife.

When the band finished the second set, the girls, my wife, and I decided to return to our tent. When we reached the camping grounds, we could still hear the motorcycle club band down in the valley. The motorcycle club had rented a generator and made a platform to set up their equipment. They didn't stop until 4:00 a.m.

When I got up the next morning, the girls were outside playing. My wife had gotten up for a while, but knowing I was asleep, she got back in her bag and waited for me to wake up. She eventually got impatient and woke me up so that I could help her with the breakfast. While we were getting the breakfast ready, I took a good look at the area around our tent. There were a number of other people around us, all white, in tents and trailer campers. The lake looked very clear and refreshing. Down the hill next to the lake, I could see the motorcycle gang. It looked as though they had celebrated a victory and were recuperating from the wild celebration. The sky was clear, and the air was refreshing; it was a beautiful day.

After we had eaten, I decided to go over to the VIP's farm to see what was going on, whether they were planning to have rides for the kids or other entertainment. When I told my wife that I was going over to the farm, she said, "On your way back, find a store that's open, and pick up some eggs and more kerosene for the stove."

When I was about a mile from the campgrounds, I saw a sign on a fence that read, "Large Eggs—35¢ a doz." I wanted to stop and get a couple of dozen, but I decided to pick them up on the way back. I kept on driving on the rocky road. On the side of the road was farmland.

There were about ten farms that I passed on the way to the VIP's farm. When I reached his farm, I saw a couple of the brothers who were in the band, standing around talking. I couldn't see anyone else. I parked the car and got out and started rapping with them. We talked about some of the things that went on the previous night and their main reason for coming up. One of them told me that if they could put on a good show in front of the rich people there, they stood a good chance of getting a rich black brother to sponsor them. One of them went into the house, and the other one told me to follow. I followed.

The house had caught on fire earlier in the summer, and the VIP was just getting the outside back together. The fire hadn't reached the inside, which was very beautiful. In the living room there was a huge picture window with a view of one of the most beautiful sights I'd ever seen. Through the window I could see the small lake, acres and acres of hilly land, with a few homes spread out, green grass, and trees everywhere. As I stood there daydreaming, I heard the door open and close. The VIP came into the house, spoke, and walked on into another room. Two more of the brothers who were in the band came into the living room. One of them had been trying to call Detroit all morning. Their driver hadn't come the previous night to take them back home to change their clothes. The one who was calling to Detroit spoke to me: "Hey, brother, could you take me to Detroit? I've got to pick up some clothes and a part that goes with my organ."

I said, "I'm sorry but I can't because my wife and daughters are at the campgrounds waiting for me, and I don't want them to be up here by themselves." I thought about calling Detroit to tell my mother and the rest of the family that they wouldn't see my tent when they came.

While we were rapping, the VIP and another guy left the house. The organ player made another call to Detroit. He was on the phone for five minutes. While he was on the phone, I decided that I would ask if I could make a call from the house. I looked for the VIP, but I couldn't find him.

He had already driven off with two other fellows. I went back into the house, and I saw the organ player hang up the phone. I said, "Hey, brother, do you think it would be all right for me to use the phone?"

He said, "Go ahead. He told us we could use the phone or do what we wanted as long as we didn't break anything. If anyone says anything, tell them that you're using the phone for me."

I called my mother and told her how things were, and I told her where I was staying. She said, "We'll be up there about seven or eight o'clock. We've been barbecuing all morning and part of the afternoon and have everything ready." I told her that I had to get off the phone because I was in the VIP's house.

As soon as I hung the phone up, the VIP came into the house. He looked as though he had a problem. He walked through the house, and when he came back, he looked directly at me and said, "Okay, you guys that I don't know are going to have to leave. I don't want a bunch of strange people hanging around here." A young white fellow and I were the only ones there who didn't have his permission, so we left. The organ player came out right after we did. I rapped with him for a couple of minutes and then told him I had to find a store that sold kerosene. He asked if he could go with me.

We found a store about two miles away. On the way back we stopped at a Dairy Queen, and I bought a half-gallon of ice cream for the family. I dropped the organ player off at the farm and headed back for the campgrounds. On the way back, I spotted that egg sign. I drove the car into the driveway and honked the horn; no one came.

I then saw a man driving a tractor and coming toward the house. He got off and came over to me and said, "Hi, there, what can I do for you?"

I said, "I want two dozen eggs."

He said, "I don't have any here, but if you take me down the road to my daughter's house, I can get them for you." He got into the car, and I drove him about two hundred yards back down the road to his daughter's house. He went in and got the eggs, and when he came back and gave them to me, I paid him. He then said, "You don't have to take me back. I'm going to stay here for a while."

When I got back to the campgrounds, the girls were playing, and my wife was inside the tent relaxing. When I got out of the car, Tina and Tammy ran over to me and started pulling on my arms and asking me to take them down by the water. My wife came out of the tent and said, "I'm going too. Did you get the things?"

I said, "Oh, yeah. I got two dozen eggs and a gallon of kerosene and some ice cream." I took the things out of the car and put them up, and then my wife and I followed the girls down to the lake. We had taken a blanket with us and spread it on the ground near the water. The day was still clear and beautiful. I lay back on the blanket and watched the girls as they played their games and ran around chasing each other.

After relaxing there for an hour, we went back up the hill to our tent. I had to leave for some water because we were running out. There was an outside water pump about fifty feet from our tent. I didn't know it until my little explorer, Tina, showed it to me. I refilled the water containers plus a small canteen that I wore on the side of my belt. Back at the tent, I played badminton with the girls and then sat with the wife, waiting to start supper.

As we sat there, I heard the strange sound of a motor. It was the houseboat the VIP owned, but there was a black man, a woman, and a little boy on it. I stood up to see. When they saw me, I waved at them and they waved back. (We were camped at one end of the lake, and the VIP's farm was at the other end.) When they reached our end, the man stopped the boat for a minute and then started it back up; he turned it around and went back. About five minutes later, we heard screaming, and yelling, and then I saw people camped on the high grounds running to the edge of the hill. I got up in a hurry to see what had happened. I knew that my family and sisters-in-law were there with me, so that relieved some of the tension. I thought someone was probably drowning. As I reached the edge of the hill, I saw four men in the middle of the lake, holding on to an overturned rowboat. I stood there and watched them, but I really couldn't understand why some of the small girls were crying, until a guy came over to me and said, "That's a damn shame. You just can't be nice to some people."

I said, "What happened?"

He said, "The guy who camped next to me let those motorcycle members in the water use his boat, and now they're trying to sink it."

Finally, after the crowd had gathered by the shore and started shouting, they brought the boat back, and one wanted to fight the owner. His friends dragged him away, but about five minutes later the wild one came back riding a motorcycle in the nude, down by the water. The people who were still there laughed at him and told the girls to avoid looking at him.

After the incident was over, we started supper. We ate, cleaned up, washed up, and changed our clothes. We then left to meet my mother and family at the farm. I didn't know exactly what time the family was going to come, but when we got there, they still hadn't arrived. The sun was just beginning to set when, finally, they came—four carloads of relatives. All of us gathered in a huge bunch and started talking. (Rapping and talking are two different expressions.) The women and most of the kids wanted to know where we were staying. I pointed to where the tent was and asked, "Do you want to go and see our tent?" They said yes, so we grouped into four cars, including mine, and drove to the campgrounds. The four men who came didn't go to our tent.

When we got there, it was almost dark. The kids were excited and thrilled to see the campers and tents. They looked inside our tent while we all stood around talking for ten or fifteen minutes.

It was pitch-black on the way back to the farm. When we got there, some of the people had gone into the bar. It had gotten cold outside under the huge tent, so we decided to pile into the bar too. We sat in the bar, looking at the different people who came in. There were a few who held a conversation, but all in all, you still had a certain few who were "too good to speak." We played cards while some of the kids were dancing to the music from the jukebox. Things didn't turn out the way we had expected in regards to rides for the kids, different singing artists, etc. It didn't take long for the smaller kids to get restless. There really wasn't anything for them to do.

The men who had come up with our family had been bored earlier, so they went with my sister's husband to Flint, Michigan, to visit his friends. Before they left, they told us that they would be back in a couple of hours. Three hours passed, and the men didn't show up. At that time everyone was ready to go, but they didn't want to leave without the men. Finally, someone said, "There ain't no tellin' when they'll be coming back." The women got together and decided that it would be best to leave. They knew that when the men returned and didn't see them, the men would call or go home.

When my relatives got into their cars and left, my family and I went back to our tent for the night. As we were headed to our tent, we could hear the music playing and the laughter of the motorcycle group as they partied the night away. It was cold outside but warm inside our tent. I had left the heater on inside the tent to keep it warm.

Early the next morning, when the sun came into view, there was a noise outside our tent. It sounded as though someone was rubbing or bumping against the tent. That woke my wife up, and she woke me up. I eased out from under the sleeping bag and put on a pair of pants and then tried to imagine who or what was outside. Someone hit the tent with an open palm. I looked for my hatchet, but before I could find it, I heard someone call my name. It sounded like my uncle's voice, but I wasn't sure. I heard my stepfather's voice, and my tension left. I zipped the tent open, and there they were. They told me what had happened, and I told them what had happened that night. I said, "How in hell did you find us?"

My stepfather said, "You said that you were camped way behind the farm. When we came back to the farm, we didn't see anyone, so we went into the bar for a while. We agreed we would look for you. It took us over an hour to find you."

I said, "The women are mad because you have all the food with you."

My stepfather said, "Well, I guess we better get on back. Do you want some of this food?"

I said, "Yeah."

He opened the trunk and said, "Get what you want." I got some food, and we talked for a while and then they left.

The noise they had made woke the kids up, but they didn't get out of their sleeping bags. It was too early for me to stay up, so I got back into the sleeping bag and went back to sleep. I woke up a couple of hours later, and the kids were up as usual. It was another beautiful day. We had breakfast together and ate. That was Labor Day, and most of the people were packing to get an early start in the traffic.

The man who was camped next to me came over, and we talked about camping and many other things. I really enjoyed his conversation. He seemed like an ideal American. After that long conversation, my wife and I started packing our equipment. We washed and changed our clothes and then took the tent down. When we had everything packed into the car, we said goodbye to the people we had met and drove to the farm. On the way to the farm, we stopped at a house across the road from where I had bought the eggs and bought nine dozen ears of corn. The people were so friendly that we talked with them for a while.

It was difficult trying to find a parking space at the farm. Cars were parked everywhere. After looking at all the Mark IV's, Eldorados, and other expensive cars, we decided that wasn't the place for us. I turned the car around and began to drive away, and then I heard someone call me. I looked, and it was a couple of brothers from the band. I got out of the car and rapped with them for a couple of minutes. I told them how I felt, and one of them said, "I know what you're talking about. We're just up here for the money." They told me where they played in Detroit and asked me to come over and see them perform. I said goodbye and was off for home.

There wasn't very much traffic on the highway. The traffic moved at normal speed. We didn't have that far to go to Detroit. When we came into that area where I usually had bad feelings, I realized that Detroit wasn't a safe place to live. I realized that I was freer in the country than in the city, even though I was among strangers. The strangers were out there for the same reason as I was—to get away from the city.

I began wondering if it was right to run away from a problem that had existed for many years. I felt that I was once a part of the problem, but I solved most of my personal hang-ups, and now I really enjoyed living. I felt like telling all the people with problems to "take a trip for a weekend, go out in the woods and relax your mind." But that would be impossible, money was a problem for most of the troubled people. They didn't have enough money to keep them out of trouble. It made me very mad to think of the position money put people in.

I came out of my deep thoughts when I reached my home. We unpacked all the equipment from the car, showered up, and took a nap for an hour. We got up and drove over to my mother's house and spent an hour talking about the trip. I left six dozen ears of corn there that my stepfather had asked me to buy. My wife, daughters, two sisters-in-law (Pamela and Sylvia), and I rode to Windsor to spend the rest of the day with my mother-in-law.

Chapter 15

The week after Labor Day I registered in college to take two more data processing classes: assemblers' language and administrative systems. Assemblers' language was a programming class that taught me how to program a computer. Administrative systems was more of a research class. It taught me the technique of how to go into a plant, business, bank, or any large organization and save the company money by putting in machines or other systems to increase production. I enjoyed the courses. The classes gave me a better understanding of the American system, good and bad. They even gave me a better understanding of people and made me more aware of the things that were going on with the progress in the nation. I had been out of school for six and a half years, but I was quickly becoming adjusted to a new type of environment. It was beautiful. I felt there would be no limit to my education.

This type of education was more challenging than high school. You were on your own; the rules were there, and it was up to you to follow them. The instructors were men and women of good will. They enjoyed teaching. They gave their respect to all the students, and the students returned that respect. It seemed to me as though they were there to teach the student, not the book. By that I mean my instructors were teaching the subject in which they were employed. They had personal experience in the subject. If the book didn't explain it well, they would explain it as a personal matter. In high school, it seemed to me that most of the teachers were there to get a paycheck.

My oldest daughter also started kindergarten in September 1972. She was very excited during her first week of school. She had heard other kids who were in school talk about the things they did in school, but she didn't know what to expect. I've always had confidence in her, and I always will. Many times, when my wife and I were reading books, Tina would get a book and imitate us. I knew that she was very curious about what we were doing. I would tell her, "When you start school, the teacher is going to teach you how to read, and then you'll be able to read some of my books." This built up her determination. I knew that she would have a better chance than I had.

A couple of weeks after school started, things began to look good. I could see that I was going to do a decent job. I had more than enough time to study, because I took my books to work, and when all my machines were fixed for the day, I would go into the men's room to read for a couple of hours. If something wrong happened with one of the machines, my inspector would tell a friend of mine, and he would come and tell me that I was needed at a machine. When I did whatever, I had to do to get it running again, I would return to the toilet and continue to read. I hated the idea that I had to hide in the men's room to read, but that was the only way I could do it.

During the fall semester I really got into the groove. I knew more about a computer than I've known about the human body. In fact, the computer is basically like the human body, but it functions much faster. Just the idea of thinking about a computer gave me a better insight into human nature and a better understanding of myself.

Chapter 16

My cousin Robert set a date in October 1972 to get married. I was chosen to be his best man. Robert had left Detroit and gone to live in Mississippi, where he met his future wife. I had never been to Mississippi before, but I had dreamed of being there. Robert, my stepfather, and many more of my relatives had talked about Mississippi. From listening to Robert tell me how much I would like it, I decided this was the time to find out for myself.

Robert came to Detroit for two weeks, the last week of August and the first week of September. While he was here, we ordered tuxedos. We ordered four, but that was a guess since he didn't know how many people from the wedding party would be able to leave their jobs for the wedding in Mississippi. Robert and I went by a couple of close friends' houses to let them know about the wedding. He knew a large number of people who grew up with him, but he didn't consider all of them close friends.

I had planned on taking my wife with me to Mississippi, but she was pregnant, and the trip would have been too hard on her. I knew the trip entailed riding over a thousand miles one way, partying for a day, and then riding the thousand miles back. About a week before we were to leave, my wife found out the doctor had made a mistake. She wasn't pregnant.

Three carloads of people left to go to Mississippi, mostly relatives. I decided not to take my wife because it still would have been too hard on her. I rode with my stepfather and three other people: Carl Hubbard, Willie Webster, and my aunt Rachel. All three cars were supposed to leave at the same time and place. It was about six o'clock when we left

Detroit, and the sun was just beginning to set. When we reached Toledo, Ohio, I could see the sky full of stars.

Driving was by rotation. My stepfather drove the first three hours, and I drove the next four hours. Willie drove the next four hours, and my stepfather finished the driving. It took us almost fourteen hours to drive from Detroit to Jackson, Mississippi. When we reached our destination, the other two cars hadn't arrived yet. My stepfather pointed to the house that Robert lived in, and Carl, Willie, and I walked over to greet Robert. Mississippi was just the way I had pictured it. In fact, one night

I dreamed that I was standing on a road, looking at the houses. In the distance I could see all the open land that Robert's grandfather owned––two hundred acres––and the few houses where all his kinfolk lived. I saw a few horses running wild, and then suddenly it started to rain. All of those visions came true, except for the rain. It was beautiful. I felt that I would do anything to live and feel like that for just six months out of the year, no matter how hard the work was.

When we reached Robert's house, there were four dogs in and around the house. Carl and Willie waited for me to run to the house, to make sure he was there. After a couple of knocks, Robert came to the door and asked, "Who is it?"

I said, "Bubble" (my nickname). Robert opened the door, and I went in. The dogs were barking, and Carl and Willie were still outside the fence. After Robert and I shook hands and he asked me where my wife was, Carl and Willie came running up on the porch to get into the house before the dogs could get them. We sat around and rapped about old times and what we were going to do that day. Robert got dressed, and all of us walked back down to his grandfather's house. Robert rapped with his uncle, my stepfather, and his aunt for ten minutes and then asked Carl, Willie, and me to go for a ride with him to pick up a few things.

As we were getting ready to leave, my sister's husband pulled up in front of Robert's grandfather's house. There were four people in the car.

When they got out, we rapped about how we lost each other on the way to Mississippi. About a half-hour later, the third car pulled up, and when the people in it got out, they joined the conversation. We finally got a chance to go to town. When we got back, we ate at Grandpa's house, and then we walked over to Robert's to get some rest before the wedding started. We were so tired that we waited almost until the last minute to get ready for the wedding. When we finally got ready, Robert wasn't, but he did make it to the church—just in time. Everything went beautifully. The weather was beautiful; it was just like summer in northern Michigan.

That evening we partied at Robert's house. It was different from northern Michigan because Mississippi had some counties that were considered dry. There was alcohol there, but it was hidden in a place where we had to sneak to get it. There were so many kinfolk there that some of us partied in the yard. While we were partying, the sun began to set. They only had a few poles with lights on them spread out in a distance, but we could still see because he had a porch light on and the sky was lit with stars. Some of the stars were so close, it looked as though you could throw a rock and hit one.

Around nine o'clock, most of the people who were there began to leave, and by ten o'clock there were only a handful of people left. The night was still young, and we were getting restless. There wasn't anything a person could do out in the country at night except gaze at the stars or sit around the house and watch television. As we sat around doing nothing, my cousin William came into the house and asked us if we wanted to go to town. We all wanted to, but there was a problem. There weren't enough cars to take all the people who wanted to go. I asked where Robert went. Carl said he didn't know. William said he'd be back in a bit. So we waited. It was only twenty minutes after our discussion when Robert came back. It seemed as though it was an hour. I asked Robert if we could use his car to go to town, and he said, "I don't know, because I was thinking about going to a motel or someplace."

I said, "Well, we might as well tell Will and them to go on."

He said, "Wait a minute." He went into the room where his wife was and said something, and then he came back out and said, "Here are the keys. Give them to Will. He knows how to get there."

William was sitting on the porch. I took the keys to him and said, "Are you ready?"

He said, "Did Robert give you the keys?"

I said, "Yeah. He told me to give them to you because he said you knew how to get there." There were five of us in the car. The other cars hadn't left when we got into the car. They pulled off, and we followed them.

It took us about half an hour to get to a club in Jackson called Club 77. There was no difference inside from some of the clubs in Michigan. The people were very friendly. There was a live band playing, and they were really playing the blues. We gathered four tables and placed them together, and we ordered two rounds of drinks. It was a beautiful feeling, sitting there watching the people enjoying themselves. We were there for two hours when all of a sudden, I saw a black man and a white woman walk in the club together. I almost snapped my neck off, looking and not realizing what I was looking at. Robert had been telling me for the past three years that the South was changing, but I never would have believed that the white and black people would be going to the same clubs together. I gazed around the club, looking to see the reactions of the other people who were there. It seemed as though the people didn't look at it the way I did. I had always heard about how black and white didn't mix in the South. I thought to myself, *I would really like to talk to an older white man and find out for myself what his opinion was on the difference between whites and blacks, and his beliefs in God.*

There was a man taking pictures in the club. He came over to our table and asked us if we wanted to have some pictures taken. We agreed and then started posing. After the lovely time we had at the club, we went to a soul-food restaurant. At the restaurant, every type of soul food you could name was served, and the restaurant was spic and span inside, with a very respectful staff.

I didn't see any fights break out while I was in Mississippi. It appeared to me that the people down there were one big happy family.

When we got back to the farm, it was four o'clock in the morning. I was feeling very good. I walked right into Robert's house, lay on the couch, and pulled my clothes off. There was a blanket and a pillow at one end of the couch. I grabbed the pillow, and the blanket fell on the floor. I didn't bother to pick up the blanket. I just put the pillow under my head and fell asleep.

About two hours later, I heard someone honking a car horn outside. I didn't get up because I thought it couldn't be for me. Finally, the horn stopped, and I heard someone get out of the car, come up the porch, and knock on the door. I waited to see if someone would get up and answer the door, but no one did. I heard my sister's husband's voice: "Hey you," he said, "whoever's going with me better come. I'm getting ready to go back to Detroit."

I heard someone in the house walking toward the front door, and my sister's husband came in. When he saw me lying on the couch, he said, "Hey, Bubble, when are you going back?"

I said, "Later today."

I heard Willie say, "Hey, wait a minute. I think I'll go back with you.

How many people are going back with you?"

My sister's husband said, "Just me and Earl so far, but you better hurry up because as soon as Earl is ready, I'm leaving. I would have left last night, but when you all came in, I was outside in the car sleeping. If I had of caught you then, I would have asked you, and if you didn't want to go, I would have been gone."

Carl then said, "Hey, wait for me."

My sister's husband said, "You better hurry up."

I lay there and thought about things. I wanted to stay an extra day, but if I did, I would miss a day of work. If I went in my sister's husband's car, there would be five of us, and there would be four people in my stepfather's car. I said, "Hey, if you wait for an hour, I'll go back with you." My sister's husband said, "If you don't get ready now, I am leaving."

I wasn't tired at that point. I felt better than I'd ever felt getting up in the morning getting ready for work. The country air made me feel so good with so little sleep.

Carl and Willie slipped on their clothes, rushing so they wouldn't get left. I hollered out the door and said, "Hey, go down to Grandpa's house and get the rest of my things, and I'll go back with you." I knew they had to go back to Grandpa's house to say goodbye, and that would give me a chance to get myself together.

When they came back to get me, Carl said, "I couldn't find your hat and comb." I took my things out of the house and put them in the car and then woke Robert up to tell him I was leaving. We talked for a minute until, all of a sudden, the horn started honking again. Robert and I shook hands, and I told him that I would come back in the summer with the family and stay for a couple of weeks. He came outside with me and shook hands with Carl and Willie and his brother and told my sister's husband not to blow his horn in front of his house.

All of us got into the car, and I said, "Hey, drive me over to Grandpa's house so I can get the rest of my things and say goodbye."

My sister's husband said, "Hurry up, man; I got to go."

I said, "Man, just take me over there. Hell, you ain't in that damn big of a hurry."

The people down there don't lock their doors. They have respect for each other's property. I knocked on the door and went right in. Everyone in the house was up. I rapped for a couple of minutes and told my stepfather that I was going back with my sister's husband.

We were finally off. We had a long journey ahead of us. It looked as though it would rain before we left, but after driving for a half-hour, the sky cleared up and it was a beautiful day. I really enjoyed the ride back because I hadn't had a chance to rap with my cousin Earl in a long time. He had seven years of college and a hell of a lot of knowledge. We got into a very deep conversation. In fact, we all rapped so long that the only one who went to sleep on the way back was my sister's husband.

As we drove through Kentucky, I gazed through the window, looking at all the scenery. I thought, *Wow, just think of the power that man possesses. I'm sitting here in this car travelling ninety miles an hour, and my body isn't moving.*

When we reached Detroit, it was eleven o'clock at night, raining, and very cool outside. When I walked into the house, my wife was very happy to see me. I had told her that our group wouldn't be back until Monday morning. I wanted to go into the girls' bedroom and wake them up to let them know I was home, but my wife stopped me.

Chapter 17

That next morning, while I was in the bathroom washing up, Tina came into the bathroom and gave me a kiss and a big hug. She asked, "Where are you going now, Daddy? You got to go to work again?"

I said, "Yeah. I've always got to go to work, so that I can take care of you, Tammy, and Mommy."

Tammy came into the bathroom and grabbed my leg and said, "Hi, Daddy!" I bent down and gave her a kiss and a hug. They both started rapping with me as I prepared for work.

My wife came into the bathroom and said, "You better come and eat. It's getting late." I ate and gave the wife and kids a kiss and was off. When I arrived at work, people who knew I had gone to Mississippi asked me about my trip. I told them that everything had gone well and it was beautiful down there. After lunch, I found out that Carl didn't make it to work that day. He usually came over to my department every day and rapped for ten or fifteen minutes. When I found out that he wasn't there, I asked Willie, "Did you know that Bug didn't come in?" Willie said, "I haven't seen him all day; he probably didn't come in." We continued to rap until one of the women came over and said that she was having trouble with her machine. I told Willie that I would rap later and went to fix the machine.

After I repaired the machine, I stood in the middle of the aisle and looked down toward one end of the building. I wondered how it would be if all human beings only had to work six months every year, with the rest of the year being devoted to traveling and educating their children and themselves on the beauty of nature. I looked at each woman at her machine, working a steady seven hours a day to survive. They probably knew that there must be something more enjoyable for them to do. There had to be something that I could do to make work more enjoyable for the women in the plant. Maybe earphone radios at each machine would provide some pleasure.

The rest of the day at work I didn't feel like talking very much. I walked around, looking at the people, trying to think of a way to make things better for them. About five minutes before the whistle blew to go home, there was a large group of people standing together, waiting to punch out. I stood in the middle very quietly and observed their actions. Most of the black people who were there were talking to friends, laughing and having a good time, but most of the white people were standing straight, like soldiers. If they were talking, they were talking in whispered voices. This didn't happen at every clock in the plant; it only happened at the particular one where I punched out every day.

I relate this situation to show that some people don't understand the difference between black and white people. The majority of black people live a life of enjoyment whenever they can. They feel they are not promised tomorrow, so they live today. The majority of white people are very conscious of themselves. They are always aware of their surroundings, and they feel they have to carry themselves in an orderly manner. I believe people are people and that they can do anything in the world they want, but whatever they do, they must not interfere with another person's life.

When the whistle blew, almost everyone was in a hurry to get out of the plant. After I punched my card out, I ran to my car. On the way home I thought about the people who had spent most of their lives working there in the plant. They were trying to make a living but were just barely making it. How long will people have to continue to slave in the factory? We were not created in the factory. Man had existed for over two thousand years without the existence of factories, but there were some people today who wouldn't be dragged from the factory. They thought it was the only way to make a living. If I had my way, I would automate factories and upgrade all the colleges.

When I reached home and walked into the house, Tina and Tammy were there waiting for me. I closed the door, and as soon as I turned around, Tammy jumped from the top five stairs and right down into my arms. If I hadn't grabbed her, she would have fallen to the bottom level. They were very happy to see me. My wife was standing in the kitchen waiting for me too.

After I took my shower, Tina, Tammy, and I rapped about my trip until dinner was ready. That was about the only time of day that we had a chance to have a family discussion. The remainder of the weekdays I was at school, studying my homework, or working overtime.

After we put the girls to bed, my wife and I went to bed and had a long talk. We talked about a lot of personal things and other things that were happening in the city. She told me that she had gotten so afraid after I had left for Mississippi that she went over to my mother's house and brought one of my sisters back to our house to stay with her. I said, "It's a damn shame a person can't live in his own home today without worrying about someone breaking in their home while they are there. It's bad enough worrying about your home when you aren't there. Something is terribly wrong, and it isn't just the black people who are ripping off the houses; it's the white people too. Maybe the world is coming to an end."

My wife said, "It looks that way."

I said, "Well, I don't believe the world is coming to an end, but I know for a fact that there are a lot of people leaving before their time. Maybe it's because they don't believe in God. There are so many people who speak of God, but no one can tell you exactly who, what, or where it is. I believe that God is in the mind of every human being. Before woman was created, God only existed in the abstract life.

"God created the suns, and from the suns She created the planets to revolve around the suns in outer space. God saw four billion years pass in one minute. God was just a mind that wandered in outer space. All of a sudden, God created life in a physical form. She created the birds, insects, and animals. This looked beautiful, but there was very much confusion; the stronger were interfering with the weaker. She created the woman in the image of Herself, only in the mind, to straighten out the confusion between creatures. But when woman appeared into this reality, her mind wasn't developed to protect herself. She had to hide from the stronger creatures until her mind developed ways to control or protect herself from the wild.

"We only exist in God's mind. That is, God's mind is all of the solar systems combined, and there is an infinite amount of them. For every star, there are planets revolving around them, but they can't be seen with the naked eye because of their size compared with the stars. Our sun is a star, but we call it the sun for identification. We are the dream of God. No one can prove that I'm wrong because they don't have enough time. We know we are real because we see each other while we are here. But when the time comes, we disappear.

"She created women in the image of herself. The reason why I say 'She' is that all my life I have always known the female to be the one to bring life into the world. I was told that a woman was three years more mature than a man. All my life I have seen how man has corrupted the system. He has misused people, created wars, polluted the air, and had no respect for his own. Women are very lovable and patient people. If a woman is three years more mature than a man, maybe she was created three years before man. If people believe that God gave the Virgin Mary a baby, they should think about God creating women first and then man from her.

"I have watched little girls and boys play together, and it always seemed to me that little girls were stronger and quicker than the little boys. I believe that life was created somewhere else in the universe and that each race had its own planet; God wanted a variety of different-looking people, as there is a variety of everything else. As these people became more intelligent, they explored the universe and came into contact with each other, and they disagreed on different religious beliefs. Wars broke out between them, and they almost destroyed each other, but they came to an agreement. They decided to take a group of people from each race and put them on this planet called Earth, but before they put them there, they took all the human knowledge from each group and made them ignorant; each race was placed in a different location on the planet Earth. The reason why this was done was to see if these people living on the same planet could survive and get along together, or solve their forefathers' complex.

"The black man was put in Africa, so when he developed his knowledge, he would have to solve his problem of thinking that he came from the monkey through the process of evolution. So he was put here first. He was given the best land, natural resources, and food to eat that would grow and reproduce itself all year. When the black race started out in Africa, it had one leader, who was the chief of the first tribe. As he grew old and his wife had many children, he had to decide which child he would leave his leadership to. When he made his decision, the majority of the tribesmen accepted it. In the chief's family, however, there might have been some distinction among the blood brothers. And if the blood brother or brothers couldn't settle their differences, the sons of the chief who didn't want to go along with their brother's leadership would gather friends and start their own tribes. This process probably didn't happen every time a tribe received a new leader, but we know for a fact that it happened many times because of the division of tribes today. This theory not only takes place in a tribal way of living, but it is the controlling factor in our family today.

"Today, man and woman raise a family and try to show each child what the parents believe in. If it happens to be a large or small family, the parents may give one child more love than another. If the other realizes it, there will be a problem between the children in the future, which might cause them to mentally separate from each other. This problem has always existed in society, and man has been trying to change his methods to avoid this problem from the beginning of time.

"I feel deeply that if a man truly believes in himself and respects his fellow man, that would eliminate most of man's problems. Every man has a mind, and that mind will interpret what the individual mind conceives.

"I've never studied our Chinese brothers' history, but I know they were put on planet Earth because they are here. I believe the Chinese were put on planet Earth before our white brothers. The white man's mind wasn't developed enough then for him to realize we are all God's children. Even today, there are some white and black people who don't believe there is only one creator. The Chinese culture is older than the white. When the white man came to planet Earth, he was ready to leave. He even intruded on the black man and put some of them in slavery to build pyramids, so that the white people could reach other planets, but they failed. They couldn't construct them high enough. If the white man could have been honest and told the black man the truth, the problem could have been worked out in a nonviolent manner.

"It took over a hundred years to construct the pyramids, and during that time, there were many pharaohs (white leaders who wanted to be gods) in command of the construction. And during that time, many of the pharaohs and people began to lose faith in their plans. The white men began believing that God put them on planet Earth because of their sins. Even the Bible tells how man tried to build a tower to reach God, but it was destroyed and all the people who were in it fell down, and when they hit the ground, they all talked a different language. The people really didn't fall down, but when they found out they couldn't reach these planets, they had different beliefs.

"Moses came and took the slaves away. Some of the white people left Egypt, looking for other ways to escape planet Earth. They had so many problems on planet Earth that they almost destroyed themselves, in civil wars and rebellions, fighting for control over their own destiny. As time passed, most of them gave up the idea of leaving Earth. They traveled westward, looking for freedom away from their own because of their different beliefs. When things got bad, the poor white man was always looking for a new world. Finally, the white man came to America and thought he had found a new world, but he found out that the red man was already there. The red man, like the black man, accepted his white brother, but when the white man with the monetary values of life followed the poor white man over to America, the rich white man bought almost all the land from the red man, who didn't know anything about the value of money.

"This was a big problem. The white man came over to America by boatloads. He grabbed all the land he could hold and pushed the poor red man into a corner. There were many wars between the white man and the red man, and many innocent people died. Finally, the white man was on top. He couldn't get the red man to work for him, and every white man had his own land, but not enough help to keep it up. A group of wise white men got together and decided to go to Africa and buy some black men, so the black men could develop their land.

But this time when the white man intruded on the black people, they used psychology on them. They knew that the black people were very religious people, since the white man studied their customs. The white man took parts of the white religion and added it to the black religion, and they wrote a book called the Bible. They told the black people that they had come to take them to a new world on their ship, and the name of the ship was *Jesus*.

"The black man didn't know how to read the white man's language, but he believed in the God that the white man talked about, so it wasn't a problem bringing the first shipload of black people over to America. After that there were problems. The bad white men had to chain the black people to get them to America. In this book called the Bible, the white man wrote it so that only the elite white people would be able to understand it. He wrote it for his own safety out of precautionary measures. 'Before the World is destroyed, Jesus shall come back again,' it says. Jesus Christ will never come back again in his original form— spiritually, maybe, but not as He was in the past."

I stopped. I caught my breath, and then I said, "Thank God for America; if we didn't come together in America and realize we were all a part of God, we probably would have destroyed the universe because of our differences.

"The black people did the trick. They developed the land, and they made the economy rise and the South rich. Some of the black minds got together and made the job easy. They invented machines to cut down on the mass slavery. When this happened, there were a lot of idle black people. So the Northern white man started bringing up black people to work for him. They gave them their freedom in order to get the job done. When the Northerners gave the black people their freedom, more and more black people migrated to the North. The Southern whites got mad at the Northern white people, and a civil war broke out between the two. "When the South started to control the war, the North freed the slaves to help the North win the war. The slaves became totally free from the chains, but the chains were still there, only this time they were in the mind. In order to keep the majority of the country populated with white people, the elite white people brought poor white people from all over Europe. As time passed, there were more wars, only these wars were called world wars. Some people think they were created to keep the population down, but I believe they were fought because of not understanding God.

"And as time passed, the population kept on increasing, and man was getting closer and closer to God every day. And then, thank God for America, the people finally realized that they were all a part of God."

My wife said, "How do you know this?"

I said, "This is what I believe. I read history books, and I look at the world and the people with my own eyes, and the story is there. Man has always been confused. When the minds came together, they didn't realize they were all the same."

My wife said, "Don't tell this to everybody because some people are too ignorant to respect your beliefs. You better get some sleep. It's getting late."

Chapter 18

I continued going to work that year, and I completed two courses in college. At the end of the fall semester in December 1972, I asked my instructor what he was teaching next. He said, "I'll be teaching systems design." I told him I'd be seeing him next semester. I really enjoyed being in his class; he was a teacher of teachers. Everything he taught about systems, I applied to human life, because life is a system. I developed so many ideas that I felt I could straighten out all the problems of the world.

Before I knew it, Christmas came. I didn't have very much money to buy all of my wife's family and my family and other close relatives anything that year. I didn't get a chance to work very much overtime that year. My time was wrapped up in schoolwork and homework. The older relatives understood, but I don't think the younger ones did. That Christmas was hard on many families.

As time passed, January 15, 1973, came. I was enrolled in college again. This time I decided to take three courses: systems design, the second part of assemblers' language, and my first college English class. I really didn't want to take an English class at that time, but when I went to register for my classes, there was a mix-up. The class that I wanted was canceled. The person who discovered the mistake referred me to an adjacent room, where there were three counselors sitting at a desk. I went over to the desk and sat down and rapped to a black brother about the different classes that I needed for an associate degree. I had been taking all the technical courses first, so that I would get a certificate, and then I planned to take all the other courses later. He said, "They won't give you a certificate until you get your degree."

I said, "Wow, I didn't know that. I was thinking that if I got my certificate, I could take it to work and possibly get a better job."

He said, "Why don't you take an English class? I'm teaching English here at the YWCA on Tuesday nights. You could get into my class." I thought, *Wow, a black brother teaching English. Hell, I know that I should be able to really get something out of his class.* I can rap to him like I rap to the brothers at work. He was about twenty-eight years old, and he seemed very concerned about getting black people to think positively about English. I signed up for English 110 on Tuesday nights at the YWCA center.

When the first week of school started, I went to my assemblers' language class on Monday. There wasn't that much to it. It was almost a repeat of the first part. The next day, I went to my English class, but to my surprise, I ended up in the wrong class. I shouldn't say "the wrong class," but I ended up in an English class with a different instructor. The instructor was a white sister. The reason I say a white sister is that, if I had been blind, I wouldn't have known if she was white or black. She didn't pull any punches. She told it like it was. She motivated the whole class. She passed out a hell of a lot of knowledge to all those who wanted to learn. She conducted the class in such a way that you couldn't do anything but learn. I didn't miss a day of class and was only late once. If I had had an English instructor like her in my earlier school days, there would have been no limit to my ability today.

The next day, Wednesday, was my day of homework and working overtime, if I was lucky enough to get asked to work. On Thursday, I went to my systems design class. This class increased my knowledge of implementing a system of my own at work, at home, or anyplace that needed some improvement. In class we got involved in company organizational charts from the chairman of the board on down. It was very interesting sitting in class, listening to the instructor lecture on the status of salaried employees. In my mind, I could see a picture of the different salaried employees who are in my shop, and I would try to place them in their proper positions.

Chapter 19

One day I saw the plant production supervisor walking through the shop, checking out the people. I decided to go over to him and ask him if he could show me the organizational chart of our company. He said, "Wait a minute. I'll be right back. What machine are you working on?"

I said, "Seventy-two." He walked away, and I went back to my machine to await his return.

Five minutes later, he returned and said, "What did you want to see?"

I said, "The organizational chart of our company."

He looked at me as though I was talking a foreign language and said, "I can't bring it out here because it's too big. When I get it ready, I'll call you up front and show it to you."

I said, "Thank you. I really would appreciate it. I'm in school, and we are studying different organizational charts."

The next day, when I saw the plant production supervisor coming down the aisle, I didn't say anything to him. I was going to wait until he came up to me and asked me if I was ready to go and see the charts. When he reached my area, I stared right at his eyes. I was waiting for him to look at me, so that I could nod my head and say hi. As he got closer, he looked at me, dropped his head, and walked right past me as if I weren't there. I was embarrassed and shocked by the way he ignored me. I decided to wait a week to see if he would get in touch with me.

Every day I waited for him, and every day when he saw me, he dropped his head.

The next week I rapped with a couple of friends at work about my conversation with the supervisor. They said, "Hell, he ain't going to show you nothing. He's afraid you might get his job." I knew he was trying to avoid me, but I didn't want to believe it.

That Wednesday, I worked four hours over my shift. Before I went home, I had a rap with the afternoon-shift foreman. I told him about my conversation with the supervisor. He said, "Shit, that man ain't going to tell you niggers nothing."

I said, "Wow, is it that bad?"

He said, "Hell, it's worse than that."

I said, "Well, I better get out of here. The whistle will be blowing in a minute. I'll see you tomorrow."

A couple of weeks went by, and I still waited for an answer from the supervisor. I was put on a different job in the same department that had the same classification and paid the same rate of pay. This job took me at least four hours to do, but I still had time on my hands. I was on that job for four weeks. One day during the third week, I got to work four hours early, and when my shift started, I was pretty sleepy. I had gone to school the night before and didn't go to bed until eleven-thirty the previous night. Two hours later my phone rang. I knew it was work because whenever they called, it was around that time. I didn't want to go to work early that morning, but the dollar signs got the best of me. At work I set up two machines, and my job was done. I had an hour to sit back and get some rest. I knew that when my regular shift started, I wouldn't have a chance to sit down and rest until I had at least three machines set. Most of the other mechanics would only do three setups all day; some would do only two.

When my shift started, I got lucky and completed two setups in the first hour and forty-five minutes. I sat down for a while, and then I went to the john. When I was through, I went back into the chart room and sat down. As I sat there, I figured I had about a half an hour more to relax before I would have to go back to work. I walked over to the side of a cabinet to get a natural comb. When I picked my hair and put the comb back into my coat pocket, my general foreman, foreman, and steward were standing right behind me. They walked me to the office, and the general foreman wrote me up. That is, he wrote on my record that I was out of my work area. The reason why he wrote me up is that the second setup that I completed was not passed, and when the inspector came looking for me, she couldn't find me.

I was probably in the men's john at the time. I tried to tell him that the room I was in was a part of my work area, but he wouldn't listen. When he wrote me up, I filed a grievance against him, saying that he was not justified. There wasn't anything I could do about his write-up except wait and see what would happen when the committee had their meeting on such incidents. I never did hear about the write-up, but it remained on my record.

Later that day, there was nothing for the setup men to do. That included me, so I went into the foreman's office and asked him if he would call the production supervisor and let him know that I didn't have anything to do. I said that I would like to go up front and take a look at the organizational charts. His eyes got big, and he said, "Wait a minute. I'll call him." I stood by the door and watched him call, and when he started whispering, he didn't whisper low enough. I heard him say my department general foreman's name. "Terry, wants to see––." He hung the phone up and said, "He's busy right now." I knew there was something fishy going on, but I didn't know what. Since there was nothing to do, I went over where there were some brothers standing around rapping, and I joined their conversation.

The next week I was called to go into work four hours early again. This time I worked on a bench; I had to maintain ten machines. During break time, I went into the cafeteria with four of my white friends.

Usually that was the time of work we could sit back and drink coffee and get into a deep conversation. As we sat at a table, rapping about life, one of them asked me if I believed in God. I really didn't want to talk about it; a lot of people get offended when you don't agree with their concept of God. I hesitated for a minute and looked at all four of them. They looked at me as if they were waiting for the answer of their lives. I started rapping about other people's beliefs that I had heard, but they didn't want to buy any of them. We sat there at the table for forty-five minutes until my supervisor came to get me to fix one of the machines. Before I left, I said, "We are all God's children, no matter what we believe in." The rest of that day at work, I managed to keep myself busy. The general foreman knew I had come to work four hours early, so he kept his eyes on me whenever he had a chance. That aggravated me. I got mad and decided to tell him that I wanted to go back on my regular job. I knew I would have to come up with a good reason why I wanted to go back. When I approached him, I convinced him that it would be best for me to go back. And after the week was over, I was on my regular job again.

A month passed, and everything was the same at work. People were complaining, the company and the union were getting farther apart, and the scrap material was steadily increasing. Management couldn't solve their problem with the workers because most of the management force didn't know how to communicate with the average union employee. Things were really looking bad.

In early March 1973, my wife told me she was pregnant. I was very happy. We had lost two pregnancies in the last four years. I prayed that this one would be a successful one.

On May 4, 1973, I went to work, and two hours after I had been there, I went to department 15 to rap with a close associate of mine. I said, "Hey, brother, I've got an idea. Let's go up front and have a talk with the new industrial relations man. Let's see where he's coming from." We had spoken to him but only on a salary-to-union basis. This time it would be on a human basis—or brother to brother. I told my foreman that I had some personal business to take care of up front. Warren and I went up front to the office and waited for the industrial relations man to give his secretary permission to let us go in. We had only waited a minute before we entered the office. Warren walked in first, and I went in behind him and closed the door. We spoke to each other and then sat down close to his desk, to make sure everyone would hear each other clearly.

The industrial relations man said, "What can I do for you?"

I said, "I would like some information concerning some test scores. I took an apprenticeship exam, which consisted of two tests. When I finished the test, I looked them over, and I had only three questions on one test that I wasn't sure of. I felt very confident after taking the test, so I turned my test in and didn't worry. It took the committee almost two months to score and tell the men their scores. They told me that I had gotten a 74 percent on the test and that I needed one more percent to qualify for an interview. I felt very bad. I knew I passed the test. There were three guys who passed that test who I showed how to take the test to become a mechanic. And those tests weren't that much different from the apprenticeship test.

"I tried to get the chief steward to look at my test, but he said that he didn't have any authority to look at them. About two weeks later, the chief steward and one of the men who were on the apprenticeship committee came up to me and told me that I missed by one percent. He said when all the guys who passed the test became journeymen, I'd be the next one on the list. They had an interview set up for me with the apprenticeship committee, and the committee tried to tell me I was low in my best subjects. I didn't believe them because they didn't want to talk to me. Each one waited on the other to say something. It showed on their faces."

The industrial relations man said, "Wait a minute. I'll look up the scores." He left the room and then came back and looked into one of his filing cabinets. He pulled out a long record with the names of the people who took the test. He looked at their scores and a committee report about their work record. When he spotted mine, he called Warren and myself over to the files and said, "Here's your score. You got a 77.5 percent on it."

I said, "Damn, I figured something was fishy. Look, how could they have made a mistake when all the names that are around me are either higher or much lower? And I know they had to look at my score more than two times because they had this list in that little office."

Warren said, "Ain't that a damn shame. How long are they going to try to hold us down? Hell, they have probably been doing this for a long time, and not only at our company. This shit has been going for centuries."

I said, "How in hell do the big corporations ever expect to have progress in this nation when they're always trying to hold people down? All my life I wanted to become a doctor, so that I could heal the sick, stop people from dying from diseases. What the hell are people living for if they can't control these sicknesses that come and go? People were created to live and then die, but they shouldn't have to suffer while they're living."

I felt like a new person when I walked out of his office. I knew that there was still a chance for the people to make a perfect world in the future, because people are already headed in that direction now. We have to stick together. The world changes people's thoughts every day. The white man thought his God was different from ours, but time has shown him the light. We are all going to die someday, so let's face reality. We were born to die, but it should be natural, not by war or because two people can't see eye to eye. You can only kill the body, not the soul. God is natural, and everything that is natural is God. Change your kids, and they'll change the world.

Life will go on as long as human beings live it. Without human beings, life would not exist to us because we wouldn't be here to know of it. That's why I said that we are the mind of God because we know we exist through the mind. The first people who came into existence might not have left any written documents of their daily activities, but they left their minds in the form of their children, and their children passed their minds down to their children, and it has become a mental process of trying to understand creation. The mind is a very delicate thing. If you confuse it, it can become a very destructive thing. People have always wondered where they came from. When I talk to people about God, I ask them what God is to them, and most of them don't have an answer. I tell them my philosophy of God, that God is everything and that God was here before people and will be here after people. God's mind is so perfect that it can imagine the entire universe going through four billion years of evolution in one second. In the middle of time, God used to watch the explosions in the sun and imagine all sorts of things. One second God saw a huge piece of terra firma fly from the sun. God slowed everything down to the point where it created many more in the process. It created other forms of life that just existed on these pieces of terra firma, and then it created people in the image of itself—that is, it gave people the mind to visualize all of its creations and understand them. As long as people exist, God will exist in the mind of people, and if the last person dies, that mind will end God's physical mind stage, and God will continue to be everything that exists. Sometimes I feel that only the scientific mind can understand this process, but it really doesn't matter, as long as every person understands that he or she is a part of God. People have got to understand that the only way that we can exist and understand our creator's purpose is to live together and respect our fellow man, and in the future, when our country and other countries get together and build spaceships as fast as they build cars, we will all be free to travel to other planets and see our creator's purpose.

It's nation time now, and there are probably enough people in this country who are ready to start this process, so that all human beings in the future will be able to control their own destiny. If this country doesn't get it together, some other country will. I, myself, would rather see this country start because I am here, and I can see that the people are coming together. This system is going to change by a revolution of the mind, and all the people in this country will be traveling around the world in the future, helping other people in the world come up to our level. It will become a free world, the way it was in the past. Everyone will respect each other, no matter what planet he or she goes to.

I went back to my department and continued my daily habits. All that day at work, I visualized how it would be in a better world. When I got home from work, my visions became stronger because that part of my better world was already there. All I needed was a spaceship the size of my home and more knowledge.

The next day at work, I was written up for reading a book. That is, my general foreman wrote on my record that if I get caught reading a book two more times, he would give me some time off work if he couldn't get me fired. I was angry all that day at work because I saw that he had caught other people reading books and papers before, and all he had done was tell them to put them away.

The next day at work, there were two engineers, a draftsman, the assistant foreman, another mechanic, and the general foreman standing in the chart room, checking some material on the projector screen. I approached the room and looked through the window to see what was going on. As I opened the door, the general foreman pushed me out of the door and tried to close it. For a few seconds I didn't know what was going on, until I realized that he was wrong to push me. I forced the door open, and he said, "I don't want you in here."

I said, "Man, move out of the way. I've got work to do." He realized that he made an ass out of himself, and he stood away from the door in shame. When I completed what I had to do, I walked over to the screen and watched all the people who were discussing the material. The general foreman was trying to keep information from the engineers. He was not cooperating with them. I knew everything that was going on between them because I had mastered the job, and I knew what they were trying to accomplish. The general foreman's attitude really disgusted me; he was against progress. He had been the foreman in my department for more than twenty years and didn't want to accept the changes that he saw coming. He had turned many people against him because of his biased ways. It was people like him who were always holding back progress because of their selfish beliefs. These people exist all over the country, in industry and government. They need help because they don't understand that we are all God's children. And when all of our brothers and sisters understand these facts, we will work for perfection, and my company and yours will be producing the spaceships of tomorrow that will give us the control of our own destiny in the future.

One day in the future, people will live in spaceships instead of houses, because this will provide them with the ability to move their entire estate in case of emergencies, like tornadoes, hurricanes, floods, and earthquakes. The ships will also protect them from lightning or any other undesirable elements.

There are brothers and sisters dying every day, and most of them who die really don't know why. In the near future, there are going to be a lot of people who will die and won't know why. But I really hope that one day everybody will know when he or she will die, because he or she will be so old that when that time comes, they will be lying back, waiting to see how beautiful it's going to be on the other side.

Chapter 20

The world changes every day. Most people aren't aware of the change. By this I refer to the mental change, new ideals for the advancement of mankind. We were created ignorant but with the strongest instrument that anyone can imagine, and this instrument is the mind. Our minds develop every day, whether or not we know it. Today we can control the development in the direction of our choice. The things that I learn from my point of view I can write down and exchange with your point of view, and we both can evaluate the content for each person's benefit. Tomorrow we will be able to gather more points of view or knowledge and use it to control our own destiny. We were created as individuals, and we will die as individuals.

As long as man lives, he will die; he is only a mind, and his mind is his worth. His mind tells him who he is, what he is, what he wants to be, where he is, and where he will go. The name of the mind is just for identification, so when a few minds are rapping about a particular mind, they will know what particular mind they are rapping about. The mind is reproduced perfectly because babies don't know right from wrong; they only learn what their environment teaches them. One day when we are all educated to understand the mind's true purpose, we will reach a level of Utopia, and the mind will be in perfect harmony.

It's going to take a long time for the majority of us to realize our Godliness. There are more people realizing it every day. But the ones who don't will have to suffer the consequences until they realize what life is all about.

I have always said that there is only one thing wrong with most people in the world, and that is their different beliefs in God. When everyone has the same understanding of God's purpose and understands what God is, the world will be in perfect harmony.

There is no God guarding over us. God is inside of us all. If one of us does something wrong, we are the ones that must punish him or her. One day we will all be doctors, lawyers, scientists, athletes, engineers, businessmen, all in one. We will all have the time one day to master all these professions because we created time.

We are only children of God. Our minds can never produce a universe like the one we live in. Our minds can only understand the universe's purpose and live in harmony with it!

Our planet Earth is in the middle of infinity. There are no walls, ceilings, or floors to infinity. No matter how far in the universe one travels, he or she will never reach an end. The only end in the universe is the end of the individual. Through scientific eyes, man has approximately five to six billion years to solve his problems—either stop reproducing or move to another solar system.

Life is a dream. If I had the power to control my dreams, I would make every dream have a happy ending! On October 4, 1973, my son Talib Steven Lake was born.

Chapter 21

Meditative Prose

Earth-Bound

I know that when my mind first came here, I thought that I was an Angel, and I came to rest. But I rested so long, I fell asleep. But now I know it's time to wake up.

Living and Dying

Judgment Day is when all men and women die. They live in that world and see life over until it reaches the point in the reality of the universe that all humans have a just and perfect understanding of what life is and what reality is all about—living and dying, two different worlds.

The Black Sheep

The black people in America are considered the black sheep of the human race. They have always sought to identify with their universal brothers and sisters. But in their efforts, they have gone astray. But time will tell if they regain their spiritual powers and unite their universal family under the power of the human race.

"To Be or Not to Be"

If we play the game of heaven right, our children will grow up in heaven before they die. Anybody who doesn't play the game right is the devil. In reality, the devil and God are the same person; it is the person with the split personality. He or she really doesn't know which one he or she wants to be. The devil is a negative person; he or she is so negative that he or she really doesn't believe in anyone. He or she does not have respect or consideration for brothers or sisters. The devil cheats; God plays fair. God will always win at the end.

Heaven

We all know that life can be wonderful. We have all had that wonderful feeling at one time or another in our life. When we put heaven back together again, the whole world is going to rejoice and feel heavenly happy. The key to Heaven is love, respect, and understanding!

Let's Make This World a United Heaven!

There are a lot of people who don't realize that they were put here to live and get along with one another and to know and not think about what God is, who God is, and why God is! When we all know what God is, together we can all live in Heaven! The truth is the light, and people must seek the truth in order to exist.

God's Children

When we speak of God, we are referring to the highest. We are the highest that we know of, but we don't treat each other like it. When the day comes that all human beings realize this fact, we will enjoy the reality that God created for his children. We are God's children, and life is our gift. It is our honor and duty to help our brothers and sisters mentally whenever possible. We were all put here together. If it weren't so, it wouldn't be. We might as well get along together, because we're going to be here until eternity.

Atoms

A lot of us are confused because our minds can only see the outside, the physicality of reality. Some of our minds have not been developed enough to see the spirituality that brought us here.

Our scientific minds have broken down matter into molecules and molecules into atoms. But no one knows where the atoms come from or how they form the features we see. They come and then they go; only the atoms know. But one thing we do know for a fact is that we are all nothing but atoms. My God is not up above me nor down below. My God is inside of me. My thoughts tell me so!

The only man who can truly say he knows god is the man who can truly say all men are brothers!"

The Queen

All women are potential queens. Every queen needs a king.

If most men knew the power of their queen, That would truly complete their dream.

What It Is!

To live. To be.

To know thyself. To create.

To go to the moon. To go to Mars.

To understand. To destroy.

To die.

Why? Everything Is Everything!

The mind helps those who help themselves! My brothers and sisters, let's make now a better day; we cannot change yesterday.

The Beginning!

Printed in the USA
CPSIA information can be obtained
at www.ICGtesting.com
CBHW020514300924
15121CB00003B/11